History of Japan

A brief history of Japan - Discover the major events that shaped the history of Japan

DINGO
BOOK CLUB

www.dingopublishing.com

"Great Books Change Life"

© **Copyright 2019 by Dingo Publishing - All rights reserved.**

The contents of this book may not be reproduced, duplicated or transmitted without direct written permission from the author.

Under no circumstances will any legal responsibility or blame be held against the publisher for any reparation, damages, or monetary loss due to the information herein, either directly or indirectly.

Legal Notice:

This book is copyright protected. This is only for personal use. You cannot amend, distribute, sell, use, quote or paraphrase any part or the content within this book without the consent of the author.

Disclaimer Notice:

Please note the information contained within this document is for educational and entertainment purposes only. Every attempt has been made to provide accurate, up to date and reliable complete information. No warranties of any kind are expressed or implied. Readers acknowledge that the author is not engaging in the rendering of legal, financial, medical or professional advice. The content of this book has been derived from various sources. Please consult a licensed professional before attempting any techniques outlined in this book.

By reading this document, the reader agrees that under no circumstances is the author responsible for any losses, direct or indirect, which are incurred as a result of the use of information contained within this document, including, but not limited to, —errors, omissions, or inaccuracies.

Table of Contents

INTRODUCTION 5

    THE ORIGIN OF JAPAN AS PER JAPANESE MYTH.. 7
    AMATERASU – THE SUN GODDESS 11
    HISTORICAL UNDERSTANDING OF THE ORIGIN OF JAPAN 14

CHAPTER 1: ANCIENT JAPAN 18

    JŌMON ERA 18
    YAYOI ERA 21
    THE ASUKA PERIOD 29
    PRINCE SHOTOKU (573 – 621 CE) 30
    THE INTRODUCTION OF BUDDHISM TO JAPAN 34
    TAIKA REFORMS 36
    NARA AND HEIAN PERIODS 38
    THE BEGINNING OF THE SAMURAI WARRIORS AND THE SHOGUNATE............ 49

CHAPTER 2: MEDIEVAL JAPAN 53

    KAMAKURA PERIOD 53
    THE MONGOL INVASIONS 61
    THE MUROMACHI PERIOD 67
    THE NINJAS 72

CHAPTER 3: EARLY MODERN JAPAN 76

    AZUCHI-MOMOYAMA PERIOD 76
    THE BATTLE OF SEKIGAHARA 83
    THE EDO PERIOD 86
    THE DECLINE OF THE TOKUGAWA AND THE ARRIVAL OF THE AMERICANS 91

CHAPTER 4: MODERN JAPAN 100

    THE MEIJI RESTORATION 100

    THE TAISHO ERA 115
CHAPTER 5: CONTEMPORARY JAPAN **126**
    THE SHOWA PERIOD 126
    EMPEROR HIROHITO 138
    JAPAN'S JOURNEY TO UN MEMBERSHIP 142
CONCLUSION **147**
BONUS **151**
MORE BOOKS FROM US **152**

Introduction

Japan, with the current population of 127 million, is a fascinatingly marvelous nation that is steeped in history and culture. Today, when a Westerner thinks of Japan, what comes foremost to his or her mind is the incomparable level of perfection the Japanese try to achieve in whatever they do.

Other things that remind you of Japan include anime, manga, gaming consoles, robotics, and yes, disastrous earthquakes from the devastating effects of which the resilient people of Japan rise like the proverbial phoenix, stronger and more powerful than before.

Japan is country of many wondrous elements including interesting and wonderful stories, people, and historical events. It is a country that gave birth to many greats ranging from the mysterious and powerful ninjas to the outstanding samurai warriors who were ready to kill themselves if they lost a battle to some of the world's most influential corporations like Sony, Mitsubishi, and more.

So, where does the history of Japan begin? Who were its original inhabitants? Who were the rulers and the emperors? This book, hopefully, will answer many of your questions of Japanese history.

However, before we go into the details of its history, it makes sense to spend some time on what the Japanese myths and legends talk about regarding the origin of this island nation that is today a nation of many marvelous inventions and discoveries

The Origin of Japan as per Japanese myth

As per the ancient Shinto religion, Izanagi and Izanami were a divine brother-sister couple believed to have created the Japanese islands and a multitude of important kami; Japanese gods and spirits. The story of the creation of Japan is narrated in the Kojiki, a mythological compendium written in the 8th century.

Before the process of creation took place, the land had no shape or form. The High Plain of Heaven (Takamagahara) was the first being to have come into existence. After this god, three primary kami including Amenominakanushi, Takamimusubi and Kamimusubi were created.

Seven generations of divine beings were created after the three primary kami. Izanagi and Izanami formed the seventh generation, and were the youngest generation of the first set of kami in the Shinto universe before the creation of the Earth. The two were assigned to give shape and form to the Earth and bring forth life on it. To help them with this task, the gods gifted the couple with a jeweled spear with magical powers. This spear was called Amenonuboko.

At first, Izanagi and Izanami looked down from the Heavenly Floating Bridge and were unsure of what to do. They then created chaos by stirring the jellyfish-like mass with the tip of their magical spear. After a bit of stirring, Izanagi lifted up the spear. As he did so, one drop of the mass that had stuck to the spear's tip fell back and solidified into the island of Onogoro.

The divine couple came down from the heavens and built a palace for themselves on this island. At the center of the palace was a tall pillar which was named the Heavenly August pillar. The two walked around this pillar in opposite directions and met on the other side. When Izanami laid eyes on Izanagi, she was so happy that she impulsively exclaimed, "What a great man!" Izanami too responded with joy and said, "What a beautiful woman!"

They then started a family and their first-born son was named Hiruko. Unfortunately, this child was born in an incomplete form. He had no limbs or bones. They abandoned Hiruko and tried again for another child. This time too, the child was not complete.

So, they reached out to the older and wiser gods for help. The gods advised that these unfortunate children were being born to them because Izanami said the first words when she laid eyes on her husband after circumambulating the Heavenly August Pillar. It was unnatural for the woman to make the first move.

Now, that they were aware of their mistake, Izanagi and Izanami returned to their palace and circled the pillar again.

This time, they made sure Izanagi spoke first after which the children born to them were all normal. The first set of children became the eight Japanese islands or Oyashimakumi.

The names of the eight islands were Sado, Yamato, Awaji, Iyo, Tsukushi, Tsushima, Iki and Oki. After this, many smaller islets and the kami of mountains, trees, wind, sea and more were born to the couple. The last child Izanami gave birth to was called Kagutsuchi, the Fire Kami, who burned her to death. In his deep grief, Izanagi shed tears, all of which became new kami. He cut off Kagutsuchi's head and more kami emerged from the bloody head and the sword.

After mourning for his wife for a very long time, Izanagi decided to go down to the Land of the Dead and do everything in his power to bring her back. After a long and dangerous journey, he reached Yomi, as the Land of the Dead was called. The entrance was well-guarded, but he managed to find an unguarded opening.

He met his wife and there was a joyous reunion. Both of them wanted to return to their palace on Earth. However, Izanami had already eaten the food in Yomi, and so she was stuck there for eternity. But, she wanted to try and convince the resident kami to give her permission to return with her husband.

She told Izanagi to stay put at the same place where they met and wait for her return. She took a promise from her husband that he would not follow her deep into the Land of the Dead. After his wife left, Izanami waited for some time, and then he became impatient. He decided to go deep inside the forest and find his wife again.

After searching for a while, he came upon his wife whose body was in a horrible worm-ridden state. He was aghast. He spurned her advances and ran back the way he came. Angry at her husband's breach of his promise and after being spurned, Izanami chased him to try and keep him with her. However, he managed to escape, and blocked the entrance to Yomi with a large rock so that his wife could not follow him.

Amaterasu – The Sun Goddess

She is the most important deity of the Shinto religion. Her parents, Izanagi and Izanami, made her ruler of the sky. After his escape from the Land of the Dead, Izanagi cleansed himself in the Woto River to get rid of the impurities he had accumulated from Yomi and his interactions with the people living there.

The Goddess Amatérasu leaving her Retreat.

Amaterasu was born from his left eye when Izanagi was performing this purification ritual. After much deliberation and battles among the gods and goddesses, at long last, Amaterasu received the blessings from all the divine beings to rule over Japan. She sent her Ninigi, her grandson, down to Japan to rule over it.

The goddess gave him three gifts including a jewel, a mirror and a sword to help him in his task of establishing his sovereignty over the land. These three symbols became the imperial regalia of Japanese emperors. Jimmu, who ruled from 660 BCE to 585 BCE, is believed to be a direct descendant of Amaterasu through her grandson, Ninigi. Successive emperors also claimed divine ancestry and therefore exercised absolute authority.

These myths and legends seem like some fairy tales with not an iota of truth to the modern reader. Yet, they tell us a lot about the historical culture of Japan. First, this story tells us about the deep affection of the Japanese people for their homeland. A large part of Japanese history is steeped in the love of the land. Throughout history, there are occasions where the emperors and rulers undertook movements to restore natural habitats and elements such as forests, rivers, etc. because each of these aspects was associated with a kami or god who demanded respect and reverence.

Moreover, the story of creation and the birth of gods repeats itself in Japanese culture, history and literature. The Japanese people learned about the importance of harmony between people and nature for a balanced life on Earth. They understood the havoc that could be wreaked if this delicate balance between man and nature was not maintained or was disrespected.

In addition, these mythical stories serve as a foundation for the Japanese belief about their emperor's divinity; a crucial element that explained many events in Japanese history, especially the unquestioned authority of Japanese emperors.

Historical Understanding of the Origin of Japan

The Japanese people believe that their country is not part of Asia because it is an island completely cut off from the mainland. However, the language, genetics and culture have obvious connections with many Asian countries.

Geologists have proved that as long as 15,000 years ago, during the previous Ice Age, Japan was connected to Asia via several bridges of land. The most important land bridges were:

- One that connected to Taiwan and Kyushu to the Ryukyu Islands

- Another one that connected the Korean Peninsular to the Kyushu Islands

- A third one that connected the Siberian mainland and Sakhalin to Hokkaido

Even Indonesia and the Philippines were linked to the Asian mainland. These land interconnections allowed for human migrations between the different areas, and a notable one was the movement of people from Austronesia and China towards Japan around 35,000 years ago. These people are considered to be the primary inhabitants of Japan. The period between 15,000 BCE and 500 BCE is referred to as the Jōmon Era.

The genetic evidence suggests the present day Japanese people descended from interbreeding between the Ice Settlers of the Jōmon Era and later migrants from Korea and/or China. Around 500 BCE, the Yayoi people from Korea migrated to Kyushu bringing with them the knowledge of wet rice cultivation.

Present day DNA tests appear to confirm these findings. About 66% of the maternal lineage and 54% of the paternal lineage are identified as having Sino-Korean origins. Of course, more migrations happened after that and lot more interbreeding and intermingling of genetic information has taken place since then.

Even linguistically, Japan seems to be connected to Korea more than other Asian nations. Korean and Japanese are both Altaic languages (a linguistic family belonging to Siberia and central Eurasia) along with Turkic, Tungusic and Mongolic. However, the Japanese language resembles the Korean language a lot more than other Altaic languages. Nearly half the vocabulary of both these languages is borrowed from Chinese.

The value systems and mindsets of the Japanese people are also closely related to the people of South Korea because of the deep influence of Buddhism, Confucianism and Taoism in both the countries. So, you can see the discipline and hierarchical structure is given a lot of importance, which is derived from Confucianism, and humility and politeness attitudes derived from Buddhism and Taoism. Of course, all these cultural aspects stem from China which is the reason historians call Korea and Japan branches of the Chinese civilization.

In addition to the Korea and China, Japan is influenced by other Austronesian countries such as Malay, Indonesia etc. In Bali, for example, the religion is a blend of Hinduism and animism even though the rest of Indonesia is today under Muslim influence which is a newer arrival.

Hinduism is also a more recent import from India whereas animism was always practiced in Bali. In Japan, Shinto is also a religion based on animism. Even the Japanese festivals called matsuris resemble the Balinese festivals quite closely so that some experts wonder if one was not copied from the other.

Despite radical changes brought on by Christian and Muslim invasions in Indonesia, and the deep influence of Buddhism in Japan, there are a lot of similarities culturally between Japan and Indonesia that predate these influences. Therefore, historically and culturally, Japan is connected to the Asian mainland and other Asian countries.

Let us get right into the history of this intriguing country, replete with heroic and villainous stories in equal measure.

Chapter 1: Ancient Japan

We will cover Ancient Japan in the following subheadings:

- Jōmon Era (15000 BCE - 500 BCE)
- Yayoi Era (500 BCE – 250 BCE)
- Yamato Era (250 BCE – 710 CE)
- The Nara and the Heian Periods (710 CE – 1185 CE)

Jōmon Era

This period is typically placed anywhere between 15000-10000 BCE and 500 BCE. Archaeological findings have shown that humanoids might have lived in these Japanese regions from 200,000 BCE when the islands were connected to the Asian mainland.

Some scholars do not agree on such an early date. However, nearly all experts conclude that around 35000 BCE, homo-sapiens migrated from south-eastern and eastern Asia to what we see today as Japanese islands. These early settlers were hunters, gatherers and stone tool-makers.

Human fossils, stone tools and inhabitation sites from this period have been excavated from all over Japan. The term

Jōmon refers to the cord-marked clay figures and vessels excavated from Japan. These markings were made with sticks after which cords were tied around them.

Ainu people celebrating, Japan
(antique wood engraving)

Initial Jōmon Period (10000 BCE – 4000 BCE) - Most experts accept that by around 10000 BCE, a stable living pattern resembling the Mesolithic or the Neolithic culture was established in Japan. The present-day Ainu aboriginals of Japan who are believed to be the direct descendants of the people of the Jōmon Era have left behind the most discernible archaeological records and evidence.

Jōmon pottery is considered to be the oldest pottery in the world dating back to 11000 BCE. The earliest stone tools referred to as Imamura are also from the Jōmon Era. Even as far back as the 11th millennium BCE, the Jōmon people were able to create pottery with sophisticated and stylish markings drawn with sticks and then impressed with un-braided and braided cords.

The existence of delicate pottery translates to a sedentary lifestyle as these pieces of pottery would have been useless for always-on-the-move hunter-gatherers. Therefore, the people of the Jōmon Era are one of the earliest human tribes used to a sedentary or semi-sedentary lifestyle.

The people used ground stone tools, chipped stone tools, bows and traps, and were probably fishermen living in the coastal area or partial hunter-gatherers. They lived in caves and practiced elemental agriculture; one of the primary reasons for archaeological and anthropological experts to believe that the early forms of agriculture took place in Japan. These early forms of farming existed in Japan around 10000 BCE, nearly two centuries before making their appearance in the Middle Eastern regions.

Early to Final Jōmon Period (4000 BCE – 500 BCE) – A huge number of discoveries attributable to the period between 4000 BCE and 2000 BCE reveal that there was a big population explosion in Japan during this time. The excavations from this period reveal beautiful and sophisticated flamed clay pots and vessels.

This early-middle Jōmon period aligns with the prehistoric thermal optimum; a condition conducive to population growth. Around 1500 BCE, the climates cooled considerably impacting population growth clearly reflecting the fewer number of archaeological finds attributable to this final Jōmon period.

By the final stages of the Jōmon period, cultivation had become far more sophisticated in the form of rice-paddy cultivation. Additionally, evidence of government control and other finds point to the fact that there must have been a migration from the South Pacific and north Asian areas which resulted in an intermingling of cultures.

Yayoi Era

The Jōmon Era in Japan finishes somewhere between 500 BCE and 400 BCE. The era between 500 BCE and 250 BCE is known as the Yayoi period which flourished from northern Honshu to southern Kyushu. The name Yayoi refers to that part of Tokyo where archaeological findings were made relating to that period. Modern archaeological discoveries reveal that the Yayoi period could have started as early as 900 BCE.

This part of Japanese history has two starting points; either the growing of rice in paddy fields or new Yayoi earthenware style. There is still no clarity on the origins of the people of this period. Some historians believe that these people were migrants from Korea. However, a more accepted version is that these people were a race that descended from people of the Jōmon period, perhaps with intermingling and interbreeding with new migrants from Korea, Laos, and other accessible Asian regions.

Interestingly, the pottery of the Yayoi period was far less decorative than that of the Jōmon period even though the process of production had become more technically advanced, thanks to the invention of the potter's wheel. The Yayoi created bronze-based items including non-functioning ceremonial bells, weapons and mirrors. By the beginning of the 1st century, they started using iron to make weapons and agricultural tools.

The society became more complex as the population increased. People gained wealth through land acquisition and grain accumulation, which, in turn, brought in different social classes. Wet rice cultivation required immense labor resulting in an increasing number of people moving into large village agrarian-based settlements. Unlike China, Japan did not have a central government or authority to control the entire region. Instead, local social and political developments became the norm.

We get written information about the Yayoi period from Chinese sources. Chinese historians made written records of Wa (which is what they called Japan) as early as 257. They described Japan as a land consisting of scattered tribes and communities and confirm that it was not unified.

The Chinese writings of the 3rd century describe the people of Wa as follows:

- They ate fish, rice, and raw vegetables served on wooden trays and bamboo
- The society members shared a vassal-master relationship
- Tax collection existed
- There were provisional markets and granaries
- They clapped their hands during worship (this gesture is followed in Shinto shrines even today)
- There were violent succession struggles in the communities and tribes
- They observed mourning and buried their dead
- Interestingly, a female ruler named Himiko flourished during this time. She was the spiritual leader of an early political federation named Yamatai. Her brother handled the state affairs, which included maintaining diplomatic relationships with the Kingdom of Wei in China, which existed between 220 and 265 CE.

Yamato Period

This period is also referred to as the Kofun Period, during which time, the Japanese Imperial Court ruled from the Yamato Province, the modern-day Nara prefecture. Although the entire period from 250 BCE to 710 CE is referred to as the Yamato Period, the Yamato clan did not have a big advantage until the beginning of the 6th century.

Until the 6th century, the clans from Bitchu and Bizen provinces (modern-day Okayama prefecture) were continuously challenging the supremacy of the Yamato clan; the primary reason for many historians to refer to this period in Japanese history as Kofun Period instead of the more clan-based nomenclature of Yamato. Kofun is the name given to the characteristic archaeological keyhole-shaped burial mounds pertaining to this period that were excavated all over mainland Japan.

The Yamato Period is further classified into:

- The Kofun Period (between 250 BCE and 538 CE)
- The Asuka Period (between 538 CE and 710 CE)

The Kofun Period

Until recently, the Koreans claimed that they took the concept of civilization, rice cultivation and the use and breeding of horses to Japan during the early Kofun before which Japan was home only to the hunter-gatherers such as Malayo-Polynesian and Ainu people of the Jomon period. This claim was perhaps based on the fact that Emperor Kammu's (who ruled Japan during the 8th century) mother was of Baekja descent.

However, modern archaeological findings, radiocarbon dating and understanding Chinese and Japanese classical texts have proven it was the Jōmon people who formed settlements and created agrarian lifestyles with little or, perhaps some, influence (especially interbreeding) from outside settlers.

This period is considered to be the beginning of attempts to unify Japan into a cohesive region. By the end of the 5th century, the Yamato clan had a distinctive advantage over other neighboring clans. Each clan was headed by the eldest patriarch who had religious rights to worship the kami of the clan for welfare and prosperity.

The power regions in Japan during the Kofun period developed in the highly fertile plains of Kinai. The capital was shifted from one place to another for a long time. However, by the end of the 5th century, the Yamato was able to gain control over the entire region and ruled from its capital at Yamato, which is present-day Nara Prefecture.

The Yamato clan's supremacy extended from the Kinai Plains to Kyushu although Hokkaido, Kanto and Tohoku were not under their control.

Kofun Tombs – These tombs were built for the members of the ruling class between the 4th and the 7th centuries. The Kofun Period takes its name from these mound-like keyhole-shaped tombs. These distinctive earthen mounds reflect rich funerary rites and customs practiced at that time.

Kofun Tombs

These burial mounds housed big stone chambers, and some of the tombs had moats built around them. The most basic shape was a square or a circle. However, the distinctive shape was that of a keyhole. Some of these tombs are natural hills, which may have been sculpted to shape. There have been various sizes of kofuns unearthed ranging from a few meters in length to some being over 400 meters in length. Toward the end of the Kofun period, these tombs were also built for commoners and were not exclusive to the ruling class.

The Asuka Period

This period lasted from 538 CE to 710 CE and was marked by the entry of Buddhism from China into Japan. The Yamato clan had become very powerful during this time. The name is derived from the Asuka region (south of present-day Nara Prefecture) within which numerous imperial capitals were established during that time.

This period is also reflective of multiple artistic, political, and social transformations that took place in Japan. The art style that evolved during the Asuka Period is called the Tori style after Kuratsukuri Tori, a famous sculptor whose family emigrated from China.

Prince Shotoku (573 – 621 CE)

Also popularly referred to as the founder of Japan, Prince Shotoku played an important role in spreading Chinese influence including Buddhism throughout the country. His name is recorded in the 8th Japanese writings; the Kojiki and the Nihon Shoki. He was the nephew and a trusted regent of Empress Suiko.

Prince Shotoku Hall, Narita-san Shinshoji Temple, Narita, Japan

He was a wise man who wanted to create a harmonious society in Japan. He was well-read and was highly influenced by Chinese writings and philosophies. This royal member was treated on par with Lord Buddha who was dedicated to creating a unified and harmonious Japan based on Buddhist teachings.

As per Shinto beliefs, he was worshipped as a kami, and even though he was not a direct ruler, the Imperial Court promoted him as a national hero and an imperial ancestor. He is so popular even in modern Japan that he has appeared on Japanese currency notes more often than any other figure. His other contributions include:

- Establishment of the Seventeen Article Constitution in 592 CE – which contained the political and moral principles to be followed by the rulers and the commoners

- Creation of a centralized government based on the Chinese government – Prince Shotoku brought together all the priest-chiefs of the various clans under this central authority

- Built roads and highways, adopted the Chinese calendar, compiled court chronicles

Prince Shotoku and Buddhism – He is considered one of the most important figures during the Asuka Period.

Known as the 'Father of Japanese Buddhism,' Prince Shotoku built many large Buddhist temples including Horyu-Ji near Nara, Ikarugadera Temple and the Shitennoji Temple in modern-day Osaka. He also made Buddhism the state religion of Japan.

In addition to making Buddhism the state religion, he sent Japanese monks to China and other countries to study the religion, and brought artisans from Korea to build temples, arts and sculptures associated with Buddhism. Many more temples were built and numerous Japanese monks were publicly ordained after they completed their studies.

He composed commentaries on various Buddhist scriptures such as the Lotus Sutra, the Sutra of Queen Srimala and the Vimalakirti Sutra. Buddhism talks about rebirth and the transient and cyclical nature of life and death. With the spread of Buddhism and its acceptance in Japan, the kofun tombs lost their relevance and, with time, they became completely unused.

During the Asuka period, the Yamato clan became synonymous with Japan as their rulers suppressed all other clans and conquered agricultural lands. While most of the people during the Asuka period were farmers, professions such as fishing, weaving, pottery, artisans, ritual specialists, and armorers also flourished.

Prince Shotoku and Confucianism – He was also deeply influenced by the Confucian philosophy, which declared that any sovereign ruled over the land only through the will of a supreme force. He employed Confucian models, hierarchical structures and ranks to bring order to a chaotic and scattered nation. However, he based his rule and governance on Buddhist teachings.

The Seventeen Article Constitution was based on Confucian principles that seek to bring order and harmony in a society. Some of the tenets laid down in the Seventeen Article Constitution of Prince Shotoku include:

- Quarrels should be avoided and harmony should be valued

- Three treasures including the Buddha, the Buddhist Law and the Buddhist Priesthood should be respected

- Everyone should obey the rules laid down by the sovereign who was like the Heaven upon which the vassals bear up to, as does the Earth

- The officials and ministers of the state must behave appropriately and in an orderly manner because they are setting an example for the vassals and the commoners

- Legal complaints had to be dealt with impartially; reward the good people and punish the evil people

The Introduction of Buddhism to Japan

While the epithet 'founder of Japanese Buddhism' is given to Prince Shotoku, the religion had already made an entry into the country even before his time. Let us look at how Buddhism was introduced into Japan.

Buddhism was introduced into Japan in 538 CE when the ruler of the Korean Baekje Dynasty presented Emperor Kimmei with a dazzling image of Lord Buddha along with some Buddhist scriptures.

The Japanese people and nobles resisted the entry of Buddhism into their land because of their inherent xenophobic nature. Moreover, Shinto was the powerful and native religion of Japan with a long history dating back to ancient times, and the Shinto purists did not like to bring a new religion into their country. Specifically, the more orthodox Nakatomi and Mononobe clans did not want to accept Buddhism

However, the Soga clan favored Buddhism because they believed that it could have a syncretic effect on their existing Shinto faith by enriching it further. Then, it was left up to Prince Shotoku to spread and popularize Buddhism towards the end of the 6th century.

One of the articles of Prince Shotoku's Seventeen Articles Constitution was 'to respect and revere the Three Treasures including the Buddha, the Buddhist Law (Dharma), and the Buddhist Priesthood (Sangha).' This article gave an imperial boost to Buddhism in Japan. Other methods of popularizing Buddhism were through the construction of numerous temples and promoting Buddhist art and architecture.

Taika Reforms

In 645, Kotoku Tenno succeeded Prince Shotoku and continued to strengthen the imperial power of Yamato over the other clans. It was during this time when clan states were converted into provinces, and the Taika Reforms were laid down. Kotoku Tenno was ably supported by Nakatomi no Kamatari who went on to lay the foundations of the Fujiwara clan in Japan which lasted until the rise of the samurai in the 11th century.

The Code of the Taika Era or the Taika reforms were based on Chinese political and economic models. Under the new Taika system, land was redistributed among the peasants of Japan. It also had a new tax system in place. These reforms resulted in the direct extension of the imperial family and their successors' powers across the whole of Japan.

Some of the now-conventional reforms under the Taika code were set up later on. However, during this period under the able stewardship of Kotoku Tenno along with meticulous planning and implementation efforts of Nakatomi no Kamatari, the Taika Era laid its powerful foundations in Japan.

The Taika reforms were set in motion within days of Kotoku Tenno's succession to the throne and a large number of codes were implemented within the first year itself. The reforms started with a few important imperial articles with various tenets including:

- All private ownership of land and people was abolished
- New military and administrative organizations which reported directly to the emperor were set up in all the provinces and the capital
- A census was introduced based on which land will be redistributed among the peasants
- A new and fairer tax system would be set up and implemented

All the members of the imperial family, nobles, and peasants surrendered their land. The census was set up which included not only land and population data but also information about the nature and amount of land usage. The census date facilitated the establishment and implementation of new and equitable taxation reforms. However, not all the results of this reform were good. The effects were felt during the later years comprising of the Nara and Heian Eras.

Nara and Heian Periods

Overview

In 710 CE, the Japanese capital became firmly established at Nara. Like many elements in Japan, Nara was also highly influenced and modeled after the Chinese capital. The capital had large Buddhist temples and monasteries. In fact, the Buddhist religious leaders became so powerful and influential that the capital was shifted to Nagaoka in 784 to reduce their impact on the workings of the imperial court. In 794, again the capital was shifted to Heian (present-day Kyoto), which remained Japan's capital for over 1000 years after this.

A distinctive feature of the Nara and Heian Periods is the gradual but certain reduction of Chinese influence over Japan. The ideas that were originally imported from China were given a Japanese flavor through changes, additions or deletions. For example, numerous government departments were established in addition to the ones influenced by the Chinese models.

Artistically too, Japan's art gained unique distinctions that were different from Chinese copies. A new Japanese language based on Kana syllables paved the path for Japanese literature. Also, many imported sects of Buddhism were given a Japanese touch.

The Taika Reforms failed in many ways, but the worst one was connected to the tax aspects. Taxes were so high that over time farmers became impoverished and had to sell their land and then work for landlords who had large tracts of land. Additionally, under the Taika reforms, many Buddhist monasteries and aristocrats got a lot of tax immunity. All of these effects resulted in lowered state income, and slowly but surely, the political and social control moved from the aristocracy to wealthy landowners.

The Fujiwara clan controlled Japanese politics during the Heian period which ran for several centuries. They employed smart political moves including acquiring crucial positions in the Imperial Court at Kyoto and through strategic intermarriages. In the year 1016, the power of the Fujiwara clan reached its peak under Fujiwara Michinaga after which its influence in Japan began to descend.

They could not control the law and order situation in the country, and many large landowners started hiring samurai to protect their lands setting the tone for the rise of samurai power. The Fujiwara clan ended in 1068 when the newly installed emperor, Go-Sanjo, decided to rid the Imperial Court from their clutches. The clan failed to control the new emperor.

In 1086, Go-Sanjo gave up the throne but continued to hold the reins from behind the scenes which became a new form of governance called the Insei Government. The emperors from this period extended control over Japan until 1156.

**Miyajima: Statue of Taira No Kiyomori,
12th century military leader, at the shore of Miyajima Island.**

In the 12th century, two powerful families held control over Japan, the Genji or Minamoto family and the Heiki or the Taira. In fact, the Fujiwara clan was overthrown in 1156 by Taira Kiyomori. Members of this clan replaced all the important political held by the Fujiwara clan in south Japan.

The Minamoto clan had already gained military power and had many parts of the Honshu under the control of Japan during the Early Nine Years War between 1050 and 1059. Again, in the Later Three Years War between 1083 and 1087, the Minamoto clan continued to increase their hold over these parts of Japan.

After the fall of the Fujiwara clan in 1156, war broke between the Minamoto and Taira families for control over Japan in which Taira Kiyomori emerged victorious and reigned from 1168 to 1178. Kiyomori had to fend off not only the rival Minamoto clan but also the Buddhist monasteries, which were increasingly taking on a militaristic outlook. All this rivalry led to frequent wars resulting in the absence of law and order and peace for the people of the country.

After Kiyomori's death, the Minamoto and Taira clans fought a deciding war which lasted for five years from 1180 to 1185 at the end of which, the former reigned supreme, and Minamoto Yoritomo became the ruler of Japan, and set up the first shogunate which will be discussed as part of Medieval Japan chapter.

Important Events in the Nara Period

The Nara Period covers the period between 710 CE and 784 CE with its capital at Nara or Heijokyo. During this period, Shintoism was the major religion followed by most Japanese, especially the working class. Life revolved around villages for the commoners who worshipped nature and kami.

Nara was inspired by the Xian, the capital city of the Chinese Tang Dynasty. The upper class in Japan copied the Chinese in many ways including adopting their written characters called kanji and Buddhism as their religion.

Kojiki and Nihon Shoki - It was during the Nara period that the Imperial Court made concerted efforts to record and document the history of Japan until that time; another element borrowed from China which had been recording history for centuries now. Kojiki and Nihon Shoki were the first Japanese literature produced during this time. Kojiki was completed around 710-711 CE under Empress Gemmei and Nihon Shoki was completed in 720 CE under the supervision of Prince Toneri.

Combining mythology and history, these two texts talk about the supremacy of the Imperial Court and the divine lineage of the emperor. Kojiki and Nihon Shoki sent a clear message to the Japanese people as well as the neighboring states, especially to Korea and all-powerful China, of its powerful history and strength. Kojiki and Nihon Shoki talked about the mythical origins of Japan and elaborated the contribution of different clans to the growth and development of the country including their efforts to unify it.

There were a good amount of economic and administrative reforms as well during the Nara period. Efficiency of tax collecting mechanism improved, infrastructure in the form of interlinking roads was laid, and coins were minted regularly. But, outside the capital region of Nara, there was little or no commercial activity. Moreover, the Taika reforms had failed and their effects were beginning to be felt now.

Shoen or the landed estates institution grew in popularity as demand for landholding increased. The local administration got more control as the old tax system failed and people began to sell or abandon their land to pay taxes and/or to meet their survival needs. The people who lost their land like this became the 'wave people' or the Ronin. These free and private people were employed large landholders for protection and security.

At the imperial court, in the meanwhile, factional fighting continued right through the Nara period. Leading families like the Fujiwara clans along with the Buddhist monasteries contended with each other for supremacy. There was a lot of chaos and the law and order situation for the public was dismal.

The Imperial Court abandoned centralization and allowed each district to have its own private militia to manage the law and order situation within its territory. The Nara period, despite many economic and administrative reforms, came to be associated with decentralized of power more than anything else.

In 784, in a bid to get back authority, the rulers moved the capital from Nara to Nagaoka and then to Heiankyo or Heian in 794. Heian (which later became famous as Kyoto) was to remain the capital of Japan for more than 1000 years after this.

Permanent Establishment of Buddhism – Another important cultural event that took place during the Nara period is the permanent establishment of Buddhism in Japan. Buddhism was introduced in the country in the 6th century but received mixed responses.

Emperor Shomu who reigned over Japan between 724 CE and 749 CE openly embraced Buddhism and gave the religion an imperial stamp. Emperor Shomu married a Fujiwara commoner, and they were both ardent Buddhist followers. Buddhism was actively promoted during the time of Emperor Shomu declaring himself as the 'Servant of the Three Treasures' mentioned in the 17-Constitution of Prince Shotoku.

Todaiji Temple

Todaiji Temple is a World Heritage Site that houses Japan's largest statue of Buddha. Todaiji Temple, also known as the Eastern Great Temple, houses Japan's largest statue of Buddha and the world's largest bronze statue of Buddha. It is one the main tourist attractions in West Japan.

Emperor Shomu constructed the huge Todaiji Buddhist temple, which held a 16 m high gilt-bronze statue of Buddha Dainichi or the Great Sun Buddha, which was identified with the Shinto Sun Goddess. From this point onward, there was a gradual but sure syncretism between Buddhism and Shintoism, which continues even to this day where the modern Japanese follow Buddhist and Shinto faiths with equal fervor.

Important Events in the Heian Period

The Heian Era in Japanese history covers the period from 794 CE to 1185 CE. Emperor Kammu moved the capital to Heian to not only get back the partially lost central authority but also for strategic geopolitical reasons. Heian was easily accessible by riverways (which were connected to the seas) as well as through land.

The Nara culture continued during the earlier part of the Heian period (between 794 and 967 CE). For example, the design of Heian was also copied from the Chinese Tang Dynasty capital of Xian though on a much larger scale. Emperor Kammu sensibly chose not to bring in any drastic reforms, which resulted in decreased political struggles, which, in turn, made him one of the most impactful Japanese rulers.

Emperor Kammu waged numerous military offensives against the Emishi or the Ebisu, the warrior clans of the northeastern part of Honshu, who were believed to be the descendants of the Jōmon people. In 797, he appointed a military commander under the title of seii taishogun or shogun for short to wage military offensives against the Ebisu people.

By 801, the shogun had won the war against the Ebisu and also extended the dominion of the emperor to the eastern parts of Honshu as well. The imperial control over these parts remained tenuous throughout the Heian period. Heian finally achieved stability when the power was concentrated on one clan again. This time it was the Fujiwara Clan.

By the 9th century, the Fujiwara clan gained control in the Imperial court through intermarriages and occupying key political positions. The Fujiwara clan became all-powerful and the emperor remained nothing more than a puppet. Many rulers did try to overthrow the Fujiwara clan but failed because of their deep pockets and even deeper political and strategic connections.

Emperor Daigo (897 CE – 930 CE) managed to rule directly without being influenced excessively by the Fujiwara clan. However, their power was not diminished even during his time. On the contrary, the Fujiwara clan made itself even more invincible by forming alliances with other influential families and Buddhist monasteries.

By the beginning of the Heian period, the shoen got legal status and the major religious institutions got tax waivers for perpetuity. In addition, these religious institutions also got immunity from government inspection and checks. Many people found it profitable to transfer their land titles to shoens in return for a part of the harvest. The imperial court was slowly losing control over land and its people.

After Emperor Daigo's time, the Fujiwara clan took complete control of the imperial court and, by the end of the 10th century, Fujiwara Michinaga, one of the most popular figures in that period of Japanese history, was able to dethrone and enthrone emperors at will. The entire administration of Japan was handled through the private administration of the Fujiwara family.

The Fujiwara family patronized and presided over many artistic and cultural changes in Japan. This was the time when many elements imported from China were given a distinctive touch. Some of the major changes that happened under the Fujiwara control include:

- The Chinese written characters (kanji) were supplemented by Japanese writing in the form of kana script which evolved into the vernacular Japanese language and literature.

- Interestingly, women in the Imperial court were responsible for Japanizing the kanji characters considering that they were not exposed to be trained in the Chinese language as the men of the court had been. Fiction and novels were all written by the women of the court.

- Other art forms such as Japanese-style paintings inspired from court life and stories taken from shrines and temples also flourished under the patronage of the Fujiwara family.

- The taiko code lapsed and family administrations became public institutions. The Fujiwara clan, being the richest and most powerful family, governed Japan in a hereditary way just as the emperor

- State and family affairs were all intermingled

- Land management was the most important occupation of the aristocracy

The Beginning of the Samurai Warriors and the Shogunate

The samurai was a warrior class that arose after the Taika Reforms of 646 CE. One of the biggest fallbacks of the Taika reforms is that the small farmers had to sell or abandon their land because of high taxes. Instead, they worked as tenant farmers under big landlords. A European-like feudal system emerged in the politico-social fabric of Japan as these big landlords accumulated more and more land. These rich feudal lords hired the 'bushi' or the first set of samurai warriors to defend their land and protect their riches.

Initially, the samurai were either members of the rich landlord's family, or were hired swordsmen who were financially dependent on their masters. For the samurai, loyalty to the master came above loyalty to his own family. During the 10th century, the Heian emperors' control extended only over the urban parts of Japan until it remained only in the capital city of Heian. The law and order situation in the rural areas was in doldrums as the emperor's police force had no control here. This samurai warrior class filled the vacuum.

By the early 1100s, these warriors gained a lot of political and military power over much of Japan. By 1156, the Heian period finished when one of the last Fujiwara ruler, Emperor Toba, died without leaving a clear heir to the throne. His two sons were engaged in a bitter civil war, the Hogen Rebellion of 1156, from which neither of them emerged victorious. The imperial court lost all of its powers.

During the Civil War, the Taira and the Minamoto clans rose to prominence and they fought for control. The Heiji Rebellion of 1160 was the deciding battle when the Taira clan established the first samurai-based shogunate government. The Minamoto clan were banished from Heian, which was now referred to as Kyoto.

The Samurai Code

The discussion of samurai warriors is incomplete if we do not talk about the samurai code. So, here are the eight virtues that define a samurai warrior.

Justice or Rectitude – is the most powerful virtue of a samurai. The samurai definition of rectitude is, 'the personal power to decide on a particular course of action based on objective reasoning and then follow it through without wavering.' This virtue helps a samurai to strike when it is time to strike, and to die when it is time to die.

Courage – Courage is doing what is right. The samurai code discerns between courage and bravery. Courage goes deeper than bravery because you should exercise it only in the cause of rectitude and righteousness. Seeing what is right and not doing it reflects a lack of courage.

Mercy or Benevolence – A person who has been trained and given the power and temerity to kill is also expected to show mercy and benevolence when required in equal measure. Magnanimity, love and affection for others, pity and sympathy are all traits of benevolence. Confucius states that the highest ruler of men must have limitless mercy and benevolence.

Politeness – Again, politeness and courtesy are rooted in the concept of benevolence. Even today, the Japanese people are known for their distinctive attitude of politeness and courtesy; an attitude that has a strong connection to the power and virtues of a samurai.

Honesty and Sincerity – A true samurai looked at money with disdain because he believes that riches and wealth hinder higher knowledge and wisdom. Therefore, for a samurai, talking about money is in poor taste. The bushido code encouraged thrift as a means to achieve frugal living. All these helped a samurai lead a life of honesty and sincerity.

Honor – A true samurai lives a life of honor and dignity and fear of disgrace always hangs over his neck. Disgraced samurai warriors are required to commit ritual suicide.

Loyalty – Loyalty was a superior virtue in the feudal era where a samurai was ready to give up his life as a mark of loyalty to his master.

Self-control and character – Maintaining a high moral standard was the duty of every samurai. Right is right and wrong is wrong. The differences between good and bad, between right and wrong are all given. One cannot present arguments in favor or against these given elements. And it is a man's job to teach his children character and self-control.

These virtues are listed by author Nitobe Izano, a 19th-century writer, economist, educator, and diplomat. While some of them might come across as a wee bit idealistic and romantic, there is no doubt that every true samurai endeavored to perfect these virtues right through his life. Of course, history is rife with exceptions and broken honor codes.

Chapter 2: Medieval Japan

Medieval Japan can be categorized as follows:

- Kamakura Period (1185 – 1333 CE)
- Muromachi Period (1336 – 1576 CE)

Kamakura Period

The Kamakura Period is considered to be the beginning of the Medieval Period in Japan. This period marks the control and governance of the shogunate which was established by Minamoto no Yoritomo in 1192. Feudalism is the word used to describe Japanese society during this period.

Statue of Minamoto Yoritomo (first military ruler Shogun) in the mountains of Kamakura town

During this part of Japanese history, the imperial court, the established central government, and the emperor were all relegated to mere ceremonial aspects and the real control was held by the samurai or the bushi class. This kind of samurai-controlled is referred to as the shogunate after the shogun, the title given to the primary and the most influential samurai.

Military, civil and judicial matters of the state were all held and controlled by the shogunate, the specialized warrior class that was the true power behind the ceremonial emperor and the imperial court. The feudal system in Japan is comparable to that of Europe.

- Both were economies based on land and its wealth.
- Both carried forward vestiges of a former centralized state.
- Lords rewarded their loyal vassals with fiefdoms and fiefs.
- These fiefs had military and civil control over their territory and its people.

The shogunate differed from the earlier shoen landowners by their pervasive military powers and outlook, which was completely absent in the shoen landlords. However, the feudal system in Japan worked more efficiently than that of Europe.

Kamakura Bakufu – After defeating the Taira clan in the Gempei War, Minamoto no Yoritomo became the shogun in 1192. He established the Kamakura Bakufu or the tent government. However, since the emperor had given him the title of seii taishogun, Western historians call it the shogunate government.

Yoritomo's administration was modeled on the Fujiwara's system and consisted of a board of retainers, an administrative board, and a board of inquiry. He appointed stewards to manage the land and estates confiscated from the Taira clan. He also appointed constables to control the provinces. Yoritomo was in charge of both constables and stewards.

Although the Kamakura Bakufu controlled vast tracts of land and estates all over Japan, it was still not a national regime. The Fujiwara continued to rebel from the north. And the Kamakura could never completely control the western and the northern parts of the country. The old imperial court remained in Kyoto and had control over its own jurisdiction. However, the new rich and influential families were all attracted to the Kamakura shogunate.

The Hogo Regency - Yorimoto died in 1199, and his son Yoriie took over the reins of the Kamakura Bakufu. However, family infighting troubled him continuously and he lost control over the other bushi families of eastern Japan. During the early 13th century, a regency was established by

Yoriie's maternal grandparents who belonged to a branch of the Taira clan that had aligned itself with the Minamoto clan in 1180.

Yoriie's maternal family was called Hojo clan under whose leadership, the Kamakura Bakufu lost all power. After this, the shogun also became a mere titular head; a regent figure taken either from the Imperial Court or from the Fujiwara clan. With the emperor and his protector reduced to ceremonial figures, the relationship between the Kamakura and the Imperial Court was strained.

In 1221, a war referred to as Jokyu Disturbance broke out between the Hojo regent shogun and the emperor. The Hojo Regency easily won this war and took over complete control of the Imperial Court, which was obliged to take permission from the shogunate for all actions.

The stewards and constables gained additional civil and military powers. Interestingly, although the Imperial Court had no real political, social or judicial powers, the Hojo Regency allowed it to keep extensive tracts of land and estates for the upkeep of their royal splendor which was needed to sanction the bakufu's reign.

The Hojo Regency brought in multiple administrative changes. First, the Council of State, presided over by the Hojo Regency, was set up in 1225 so that other military chiefs could be given opportunities to exercise their legislative and judicial authority in the Kamakura. The Council of State represented a collective leadership group that everyone involved was happy with.

The Joei Shikimoku, Japan's first military code, was promulgated and adopted in 1232. The Joei Code reflected a profound transition of Japan from an imperial court to a militarized order. It also retained the Confucian values like unstinted loyalty to the master and attempted to prevent the decline of morals during that time.

This new military code laid down stringent laws that stressed the importance of constables and stewards in carrying out their tasks diligently. The code provided laws to settle land disputes and to manage inheritances and punishments for violators. The Joei Code remained in effect for nearly 650 years after it was first set up in 1232.

The Hojo clan maintained a very tight control over their regions and the slightest sign of rebellion was crushed immediately. The shogun remained in Kyoto and the stewards and constables managed the provinces loyally and efficiently.

There were long periods of peace and prosperity (several decades) in Japan during the Hojo Regency until an external power, the Mongols, invaded the country in 1274.

Minamoto Yoshitsune – deserves a special place in the history of Japan, especially during the early Kamakura times. He was Yoritomo's brother and a brilliant general whose war strategies are part of Japanese military folklore. Legend has it that the two brothers were separated during their childhood but were brought together again to fight against the Taira clan and put the Minamoto family on the Japanese's shogunate map.

However, a bitter rivalry sprung between the two brothers, and despite all the help that Yoshitsune gave Yoritomo, the latter put him to death. Historians believe that Yoritomo's jealousy, high ambitions and suspicious nature could have been the reason for the sibling rivalry. Yoritomo decided to get rid of his brother backing his decisions with treason.

To escape from his brother. Yoshitsune was forced to live a life of ignominy from 1185 until he committed suicide in 1189. There are numerous war stories of this brilliant general in the Heike Monotagari. He led a string of battles for the Minamoto clan and was responsible for the complete annihilation of the Taira clan paving the way for his brother, Minamoto Yoritomo to be crowned shogun in 1192 and establishing the shogunate that would rule Japan for nearly 700 years after that.

His war chroniclers and those who fought beside and against him have left behind stories of Minamoto Yoshitsune's valor and power of strategy. Kujô Kanezane, one of Yoritomo's supporters made this note about Yoshitsune in his diary in 1185; 'Yoshitsune left behind a legacy of great achievements won through bravery, justice, and benevolence. His name will remain in posterity. He committed no treason. The only thing he rebelled against was his brother Yoritomo.'

The story of Minamoto Yoshitsune is samurai folklore in Japan today.

Cultural Aspects of the Kamakura – Many literary works were written during the Hojo Regency including:

- The Hojoki – which reflected the confusion and turmoil of the period and presented the impermanence of all things and the uselessness of human vanity as per Buddhist tradition.

- The Heike Monotagari – told the story of the rise and fall of the Taira clan which was also referred to as the Heike clan. This book was full of stories of wars and heroic deeds of the samurai

- Shin kokinshu wakashu – was an anthology of poems; 20 volumes were published between 1201 and 1205

Buddhism During the Kamakura – The continuous conflicts and uncertainties of a large part of the Kamakura period increased the attraction for Buddhism which preached ultimate salvation as the final aim of human beings. Therefore, Kamakura was the time for the further spread and popularization of Buddhism in Japan.

The earlier Heian sects were more esoteric in nature and did not appeal much to the masses. They were more appealing to the intellectuals of the society. The monasteries of Mount Hiei were very powerful. However, they were attractive only to those people who could undertake a systematic study of the teachings.

This situation of Buddhism in Japan during that time led to the rise of two new sects including the Zen Buddhism and Jodo or Pure Land Buddhism, which were most prominent during the Kamakura reign. The Jodo sect was founded on unconditional prayer and devotion to Amida Buddha while the Zen sect rejected all scriptural, intellectual and temporal authority and instead, focused on building moral character.

The growing military class was attracted to Zen and many of them turned to Zen masters who were considered to be the embodiment of truth.

The Mongol Invasions

The Mongol Invasions of 1274 and 1281 devastated Japan withering down the country's resources and power. These two invasions almost destroyed the samurai culture and the entire country of Japan. However, a miraculous typhoon saved the last Japanese bastion from which they rose again.

Japan started the Mongol invasion on a highly positive note. The country, after all, had the power and protection of the noble, brave and outstandingly competent samurai warriors on its side. However, the brute force and sheer strength of the Mongols were too formidable to handle. These two invasions made the Japanese warriors question every honor code they had fought hard to draw up and maintain because these codes seemed to crumble in the face of the fierce Mongol invasions.

The details of the Mongol Invasion of Japan is available to us through the scrolls commissioned by Takezaki Suenaga, a samurai who fought in both the Mongol invasions.

Before the Invasion – In 1266, Kublai Khan, the Mongol king and grandson of Genghis Khan whose life ambition was to subdue the entire country of China, sent an emissary to the Japanese emperor demanding tribute or be ready to face the consequences. The message was returned unanswered. The Khan sent five more messages to the Japanese shogun over the next six years. The messengers were not even allowed to disembark on the Honshu islands.

In 1271, Kublai Khan was victorious against the Song Dynasty and declared himself China's emperor under the new Yuan Dynasty. He ruled over a large part of China in addition to Korea and Mongolia. A huge number of his cousins and uncles controlled his empire from the Pacific coast in the east to Hungary in the west.

The imprudence of the Japanese shogun and emperor angered the Khan and he demanded a strike against the island country in 1272. However, his advisors told him to bide his time until Mongol warships were ready. About 300-400 warships that held a 40,000-strong army finally attacked Japan in 1274 for the first time. The Japanese were able to garner only 10,000 samurais (and even those were indulging in clan squabbles).

The First 1274 Invasion – In the autumn of 1274, a large fleet of warships along with a larger number of small boats left from the Masan port in southern Korea towards the Sea of Japan to launch an attack. The Mongols attacked and captured the islands of Iki and Tsushima by slaughtering the 300 residents of these islets.

After this, the Mongols sailed on towards the east. On November 18, 1274, the Mongol ships arrived at Kyushu's Hakata Bay, near the modern-day city of Fukuoka. The samurai fought using their bushido code, which called for each warrior to step out, say his name and lineage and challenge the enemy camp to one-to-one combat. The Mongols did not know this code. Each time a samurai stepped forward, the Mongol soldiers swarmed around him killing him instantly.

Moreover, the Mongol soldiers had explosive shells and poison-tipped arrows that used a shorter bow for deadly accuracy. The Mongols also fought in units as against the samurai who fought singly. All these elements of Mongol warmongery were completely new to the Japanese samurai and they were no match for such fierceness and brute force.

Miraculously, the Mongol ships were attacked by gigantic typhoons resulting in all their ships lying at the bottom of the Pacific Ocean and over 13000 Mongol soldiers drowned in its ice-cold waters. The bruised and battered survivors went back home and spared Japan from being completely annihilated.

There was a 7-year uneasy break. During this time, the samurai became a disgruntled lot as they were not rewarded for their efforts against the Mongol invasion. In fact, many of the samurais were very unhappy with the Kamakura. Kublai Khan sent Chinese emissaries again to the Japanese court ordering the emperor to come to Dadu, his capital and pay him tribute. This time, the Japanese responded by beheading the emissaries.

Then, they started preparing for the second Mongol attack. They constructed a wall around the Hakata Bay. This defensive wall was 5-15 feet in height and 25 miles in length. The Japanese mustered more samurai men too. Kublai Khan, in the meantime, set up a committee in his government called the Ministry for Conquering Japan which planned a two-pronged approach to crush Japan completely.

The Second 1281 Invasion – This time the Japanese warriors were far better prepared as compared to the first Mongol invasion. However, Kublai Khan was also better prepared too. He launched a two-pronged approach; one smaller set of soldiers came from the Masan port of Korea, and another larger second set of soldiers set out from Southern China.

The Korean ships reached Hakata Bay on June 23, 1281. But the samurais were able to fend them off and keep them engaged in a stationary battle. The samurais set Mongol ships on fire in the dead of the night. They used other such tactics that they have learned after the disaster first attack. The night-time raids were able to create havoc in Kublai Khan's camp, and a stalemated battle continued for 50 days as they waited for the Yuan force to reach Hakata Bay.

The second set of Kublai Khan's soldiers reached Hakata Bay on August 12. The sheer number of soldiers and ships were so staggering that the Japanese gave up hope and were ready to be slaughtered. Then, a miracle occurred.

Japan's Miracle – On August 15, 1281, just like what had happened during the first attack, a typhoon roared into Hakata Bay in Kyushu. Kublai Khan had sent over 4000 ships out of which only a few hundred were able to survive the power of the roaring winds and towering waves.

Nearly all of Kublai Khan's men were drowned in the 'magical' typhoon and those who managed to come ashore were killed mercilessly by the samurai. The Japanese believed that the gods sent the two typhoons to keep the Mongols out. They called the two typhoons kamikaze or divine winds. Even Kublai Khan did not attempt a third attack on Japan preferring to believe that supernatural forces protected the Japanese lands.

The Aftermath of the Mongol Invasions – As had happened after the first invasion, the Kamakura bakufu could not pay the samurai or the priests who had also demanded payment because they said that it was their prayers that brought the terrible typhoons to help the samurai.

The bakufu did not have much to give. Moreover, the priests wielded more control over the bakufu and, therefore, what little money and wealth was available went to the priests. There was a lot of dissatisfaction and discontentment among the samurai warriors over the following decades. In 1318, a powerful emperor of the imperial court, Go-Daigo, challenged the authority and power of the bakufu. The samurai refused to help their leaders at this crucial juncture.

A bitter and complicated civil war continued for 15 years after this. The bakufu was defeated and the Ashikaga Shogunate took over the reins of power in Japan. The story of the miraculous kamikaze was passed on through generations and, even today, this legend is used for inspiration by the soldiers of Japan.

The Muromachi Period

The Muromachi Period - also referred to as the Ashikaga Era or the Muromachi bakufu - covers the period between 1336 and 1573. Japan was under the Ashikaga shogunate during this time. The early years from 1336 to 1392 is called Nanbokucho (or the North and South court era). The period from 1467 until 1573 is called the Sengoku period.

The Nanbokucho - The Mongol invasion did not succeed in capturing Japan. But it drained the coffers of the Kamakura bakufu. Moreover, the discontentment among the samurai warriors threatened the power of the bakufu. The Hojo Regency decided to allow two imperial courts simultaneously; one ruling the Northern Court and another ruling the Southern Court. The Hojo Regency hoped that this divisive approach would weaken the Imperial Court's power in Kyoto.

The divisive method succeeded for many generations until Go-Daigo, one of the royal members of the Southern Court, ascended the throne there. He was strong and powerful and wanted to challenge the authority of the Hojo Regency and revolted against them.

Ashikaga Takauji was sent by the Kamakura bakufu to start the rebellion. However, he turned against his masters and joined forces with Emperor Go-Daigo, and the two of them were able to defeat the Hojo Regency. Emperor Go-Daigo tried to revive the powers of the old imperial courts through the Kemmu Restoration, which he promulgated in 1334. However, the success of Emperor Go-Daigo did not last long.

Ashikaga Takauji only sided with him to defeat the Hojo Regency and not to restore full powers to the imperial court as the emperor had hoped. Takauji joined hands with the Northern court and started a civil war between the north and south imperial courts. During the early part of the Civil War, the Ashikaga placed a puppet emperor on the throne of the Northern Court and this eventually became the Shogunate.

Conflicts between the north and the south courts continued for a long time after the Ashikaga shogunate rose to power (until 1392). While the new shogunate wrestled even the little remaining powers from the imperial courts, they were not as powerful as the Kamakura bakufu.

The third Ashikaga shogunate was Ashikaga Yoshimitsu who set up his residence in the Muromachi district, which became the shogunate's headquarters. Ashikaga Yoshimitsu (1394 – 1408) was able to bring some semblance of order into the country.

Yoshimitsu enhanced the constables' powers and allowed them to become powerful regional leaders called daimyo. A power balance evolved over time between the daimyo and the shogunate. The three most influential daimyo families took turns to be the shogunate deputies.

In 1392, Yoshimitsu was finally able to unify the northern and southern imperial courts, though the northern court wielded more power than the southern imperial line. Slowly, the northern court-maintained control over the Kyoto throne.

The Sengoku Period - After Yoshimitsu, the power of the Ashikaga shogunate declined and regional strongmen, especially the daimyo, became local power centers. The shogun's decision to choose the next emperor lost value, and the daimyo supported their own candidates.

Slowly, the fight for succession within the Ashikaga clan resulted in the Onin War (1467 -1477). This war devastated Kyoto and ended the bakufu power. Power daimyo powers such as Imagawa Shimazu and Takeda now started establishing their own domains. The lands and possessions of other daimyo such as the Toki, Hosokawa, and Shiba were taken over by retainers and subjects like the erstwhile Hojo family, the Oda clan and the Saito Dosan. These new sets of regional Sengoku daimyo held sway in each other's domains and territories.

Additionally, the commoners all over Japan joined hands with the religious leaders of the Pure Land sect of Buddhism to rebel and resist against the daimyo rule forming the ikko ikki, an army of peasants, farmers, a few noblemen, and Buddhist monks for this purpose. Some of the ikko ikki groups were able to establish their own domains, the most famous one being the ikko ikki in the Kaga province which lasted for over a century.

This period where everything turned topsy-turvy in Japan is called the Gekokujou period which literally means 'bottom conquers the top.' The name is reflective of the state of Japanese society where people from the lower ranks overthrew their masters and kings to take over the reins of power. The absence of a central authority at Kyoto resulted in a period of social upheaval in the country.

This situation continued until Oda Nobunaga re-established the Muromachi Shogunate in 1568, to set the tone for the Azuchi-Momoyama period. Although a central authority restarted at Kyoto, the struggle for power between the warring north and south Japan continued before final unification and peace was achieved after Nobunaga's assassination in 1582.

The Onin War – was fought between the clans and supporters of two samurais both of whom were close to the Ashikaga Shogunate. The first samurai, nicknamed Red Monk, was Yamana Sozen, and the second samurai was Hosokawa Katsumoto, the Red Monk's son-in-law.

The purpose of the Onin War was a fight for the succession of the Ashikaga Shogunate. Each of the two samurais had a mansion in Kyoto which became their respective military bases.

The war began when the Hosokawa clan attacked the house of Isshiki, a general in the Red Monk's camp. Isshiki's mansion was just opposite to Hosokawa's mansion. There were continuous battles across a charred wasteland that lay between the two mansions, and this situation lasted for a year. A lot of new weaponry was then imported from China much of which were used in the Onin War.

This war dragged on and spread to other provinces as well. As the families were involved in battles, looting mobs moved into Kyoto leaving the imperial capital in ruins. Hosokawa and Yamana both died in 1473. But, by then, the cause of their conflict was forgotten, and the Onin War continued. It came to be known as the precursor to the Age of Warring States (the Sengoku Period).

The Ninjas

The Ninja Origins - The origins of the ninja (the proper Japanese term is shinobi) clans are difficult to pinpoint because the use of assassins and spies were always in existence. Japanese folklore attributes ninjas to divine beings who descended from a half-crow-half-man demon. Historically, it appears that the ninja class must have been formed to oppose their upper-class counterparts, the samurai.

Some historians say that the ninjas grew powerful during the years between 600 and 900 CE. Prince Shotoku is believed to have employed a shinobi named Otomono Sahito. By the beginning of the 10th century, the Tang Dynasty in China had weakened and many generals from there were forced to migrate to Japan bringing with them war tactics and philosophies.

Monks also fled from chaotic China around the 1020s bringing new medicines and warring tactics into Japan. Many of these warring philosophies, medicines and other elements brought from China had their origins in India and then traveled through Tibet into China. These monks taught their fighting methods to the bushi and the ninja clans.

The Ninja Schools - The ninjutsu form of warfare was formalized by Kain Doshi and Daisuke Togakure around the 12th century. Daisuke was a former samurai and Kain Doshi was a wandering Chinese monk. Daisuke gave up his bushido code and the two formalized the guerrilla war tactics collectively known as ninjutsu. Daisuke's descendants created the first school for ninja called Togakure-Ryu; Ryu is school in Japanese.

Who were the ninjas? Some of the jonin or the ninja leaders like Daisuke were disgraced former samurai who chose to give up their bushido code rather than commit the ritual suicide. But, most of the ordinary ninjas were from the working class of farmers and villagers and not from nobility.

These common people learned the ninjutsu for self-preservation as well as to carry out political assassinations using stealth rather than the fanfare associated with war. Consequently, the ninja strongholds were the Koga and Iga Provinces known for their silent villages and rural farmlands.

Women also learned ninja combat. Women ninjas called kunoichi infiltrated the enemy camps in the guise of servants, dancers, or concubines and were very successful spies who also undertook assassination tasks.

Use of Ninjas by the Samurai – The bushido code prevented the samurai from indulging in any type of warfare except the open type. However, it was not always possible to prevail and win with open-types of battles. During these times, the samurai hired ninjas to do the spying and undercover kind of dirty work such as planting misinformation, assassinations and spying without sullying their own honor.

This kind of work paid handsomely and a lot of wealth was transferred to the ninjas most of whom were from the commoner class. The trick in this system was that the samurai's opponents could also hire ninjas to do their work. Therefore, ninjas as a group, were feared, despised and revered equally.

There were hierarchical levels in the ninja class as well and these included:

- Jonin – the high-level ninja class who received orders from samurais or other people from the nobility

- Chunin – the middle-man ninja who took their orders from the Jonin and passed them on to the ordinary ninja

- Genin – the ordinary ninja who actually carried out the task

This hierarchy was typically based on the social class that the ninja came from before his training. However, any skilled ninja could rise up in the ranks well beyond his class of origin.

The Rise and fall of the Ninjas – The ninja class came into its own and their popularity soared during the tumultuous period between 1336 and 1600. This period was characterized by constant wars and battles in which ninja skills were extremely useful. Ninjas played an important role in the Nanbukucho Wars between 1336 and 1392, the Onin Wars in the 1460s and the Sengoku periods where they helped the samurais in their internal power strife.

During the Sengoku Period (1467 – 1568), the ninjas participated actively in all the political and military games of the nobles. They were also a destabilizing influence. During his attempts to unify Japan, Oda Nobunaga saw the ninja strongholds of Iga and Koga provinces as threats to the stability of the country. He was able to defeat the ninja forces from Koga. But the Iga forces were more formidable and he had to use a 40,000-strong army to defeat them.

After this, the ninja power was scattered although they did not vanish completely. They continued to fight on both sides of any battle using stealth and guerrilla tactics. The Edo Period (which is discussed in the next chapter) brought sustaining peace in Japan resulting in the end of the ninja era.

Chapter 3: Early Modern Japan

The early modern Japanese history can be categorized into:

- Azuchi-Momoyama Period (~1573 – ~1603 CE)
- Edo Period (1600 – 1867 CE)

Azuchi-Momoyama Period

This period in Japanese history runs between 1568 and 1600 CE and includes the governance of two important rulers, namely Oda Nobunaga and Toyotomi Hideyoshi, with Kyoto as their capital. The name Azuchi-Momoyama comes from the names of the two castles they occupied; Azuchi Castle of Oda Nobunaga and Momoyama Castle of Toyotomi Hideyoshi.

Reunification – Between 1560 and 1600, many powerful leaders arose to defeat and quell the rebellions and wars among the daimyo and unify the country. Three of these leaders are important figures in the history of Japan and they include:

- Oda Nobunaga (1534 – 1582 CE)
- Toyotomi Hideyoshi (1536 – 1598 CE)

- Tokugawa Ieyasu (1542 – 1616 CE)

As these three overlords' military and civil powers increased, each of them looked for approval from the Imperial Court at Kyoto.

Oda Nobunaga - In 1560, Oda Nobunaga successfully defeated an attack on Kyoto from another warring overlord. He marched to the capital in 1568 at the emperor's sanction and installed his candidate as the shogun. He used his military powers to control the bakufu.

Initially, Nobunaga was resisted in his attempts to gain control over the imperial court by some daimyo, Buddhist monks and other hostile merchants. He first struck the militaristic Tendai Buddhist monks by attacking their monastery at Mount Hiei in 1571. In the ensuing battle, thousands of monks were killed and slaughtered.

By 1573, Oda Nobunaga had managed to defeat and control the local daimyo and exiled the last Ashikaga shogun. This was the beginning of the Azuchi-Momoyama Period in Japan that lasted between 1573 and 1600. After eliminating all his rivals, Oda Nobunaga built a huge palace at Azuchi. The seven-story castle was constructed on the banks of Lake Biwa and was surrounded by stone walls.

This strong castle that was able to withstand firearms became a symbol of reunification. Oda Nobunaga's power and popularity increased because:

- He bought over the loyal services of the conquered daimyo by giving them free lands and estates

- He freed up trade and commerce

- He enlisted the militarized merchants and monasteries into his army

- He used large-scale warfare tactics to conquer 1/3rd of the provinces

- He institutionalized administrative processes such as organizing the village administration into a structured system, standardizing measurements and creating a structure for smooth collection of taxes

Simultaneously, the daimyo (both Nobunaga's loyalists as well as those outside of his control) fraternity was modernizing and fortifying their castles and administration. In 1577, he sent his chief general, Toyotomi Hideyoshi, to battle and conquer western Honshu provinces. This war was a long one, and in 1582, when Nobunaga himself led an army to help his general, he was assassinated by one of his own retainers.

Toyotomi Hideyoshi, a preeminent daimyo, warrior, general and politician of the Sengoku period

Toyotomi Hideyoshi – Hideyoshi killed the people responsible for his master's assassination. In return for this, he was given joint guardianship of his Oda Nobunaga's minor son along with three others. By 1584, Hideyoshi eliminated the other three guardians to become the undisputed successor of Nobunaga.

Hideyoshi was a commoner by social status. In 1584, he was adopted into the Fujiwara clan and was bestowed the family name of Toyotomi. He was also given the title of tanpaku which represents military and civil control over all of Japan. Further, he allied with three major daimyos and continued his attempts at reunification. In 1590, he won a big battle against one of the biggest contending daimyo and finally, Japan was reunified.

The entire country was under Hideyoshi's control either through his vassals or directly and he evolved a new government structure, which had Japan under the rule of one daimyo alliance, but still, decentralization existed. The basis of wealth was land. He devised a new system of land measurement, which had koku as the basic unit. One koku was equal to 180 liters of rice. A daimyo was one who held land, which could produce 10,000 or more koku of rice.

Hideyoshi himself controlled 2 million koku while another major overlord, Tokugawa Ieyasu, controlled 2.5 million koku. Iyesu was a formidable daimyo who controlled large parts of central Honshu and who was not totally under Hideyoshi's control.

Hideyoshi was both powerful and feared. Yet, his position was not very secure. So, he made administrative arrangements to his advantage. For example, he reassigned the Tokugawa family to Kanto and put his trusted daimyo around their new territory to keep an eye on their movements. He engineered a hostage system for daimyo family members in his castle at Momoyama and entered into marriage alliances to strengthen his position.

The koku system facilitated the reassessment of land in the entire country. In 1590, he banned all mobility among the social classes resulting in clear class differences between bushi and farmers. Only the bushi were allowed to carry arms. He started an orderly form of succession in 1591 by handing over the regency to his son while he took on the title of retired tanpaku or taiko. Toward the end of his life, he created a balance in the administrative system by setting up certain political bodies including:

- A 5-member Board of Regents – this board was sworn to support the Toyotomi and keep the peace in the unified nation; Tokugawa Ieyasu was one of the five members of this board

- A 5-member Board of House Administrators – to manage routine administrative and policy matters

- A 3-member Board of Mediators – this board had to keep the peace between the above two boards

Cultural and Religious Aspects during the Aruchi-Momoyama Period – Momoyama art flourished during this time. It was a period when the Japanese people were interested in the outside world. They developed large urban centers. There was an increase in leisure and merchant businesses. Ornate castle architecture replete with beautiful screen paintings reflected daimyo wealth and power. The paintings depicting the southern barbarians as the Europeans were popular and exotic.

In 1577, Hideyoshi had captured Nagasaki, an important port that connected to the outside world. He regulated overseas activities and controlled various trade associations. He requested China for trade concessions but was rebuffed. Despite this setback, Hideyoshi sent successful commercial missions to the Philippines, Malaysia and Thailand. He was, however, very suspicious of Christianity as he believed it to be counterproductive to daimyo activities and ordered the crucifixion of many Christian missionaries.

One of Hideyoshi's primary ambitions was to annex China. In 1592, he led a 200,000-strong army and attacked Korea, a flourishing kingdom that was aligned with China. His troops quickly ran over the Korean peninsula. However, later on, his army could not face the offensive of a combined Korean-Chinese force. His naval ships were crushed and he agreed to peace negotiations during which Hideyoshi demanded free trade status for Japan, a part of Korea and a Chinese wife for his emperor back in his country.

This demand for equal status with China was met with disdain and the peace negotiations ended with Hideyoshi getting nothing. In 1597, he again planned another attack on Korea. However, his death in 1598, ended this campaign.

The Battle of Sekigahara

With Hideyoshi's death in 1598, Japan was torn asunder by numerous factional wars among the powerful daimyos who wanted to control the shogunate. All these wars culminated in the Battle of Sekigahara on October 21, 1600. This battle was fought between Tokugawa Ieyasu and Ishida Mitsunari, two of the most influential and powerful daimyos.

Ishida was supported by many other daimyos because of his ostensible preference to have Hideyoshi's son, Hideyori, take his father's place. This attitude attracted other daimyos who were loyal to Hideyoshi. He had an 80,000-strong army. Since most of his supporters were from the western part of Japan, his side was referred to as the 'Army of the West.'

Ieyasu was a huge landlord and a brilliant military strategist. His castle was at Edo, a little fishing village on the Kanto plains. He also had a large number of supporters including the influential Matsudaira family. Ieyasu and his allies were from the eastern part of Japan, and therefore, his 74,000-strong army was referred to as the 'Army of the East.'

In July 1600, Ieyasu was tricked into leaving a meeting of the Regent's Council ostensibly to protect his estates from a troubling neighbor who was an ally of Ishida. The Regent's Council consisted of five members who had joint guardianship of Hideyori.

After Ieyasu left to defend his land, Ishida called for forces from his western territories to take Ieyasu by surprise from the rear and defeat him easily. However, he had underestimated the powerful spy network of Ieyasu who already knew that it was a trick to take him away from the meeting and surprise him with an attack from the rear. He pretended he was traveling in the direction of his northern lands, but turned west to meet the oncoming army of Ishida.

Tables turned, and Ishida was the one taken by surprise. He thought that Ieyasu was traveling west to capture Sawayama, one of his most powerful strongholds. Ishida thought that the only way to prevent Ieyasu from attacking Sawayama was to meet him in open battle at Sekigahara, which was close to Sawayama.

And this is exactly what Ieyasu wanted. He was an outstanding open-field battle strategist, and despite his smaller-sized army, he was able to defeat Ishida.

Effects of the Battle of Sekigahara The Battle of Sekigahara was the final step in the unification attempts of Japan. Here are some of the important outcomes of this battle:

- New sets of political relationships emerged which remained in force for nearly 2 ½ centuries which brought in a long period of peace and prosperity

- The Toyotomi's claim for supremacy was almost decimated

- Tokugawa Ieyasu became the undisputed shogunate and he was appointed to the post officially by the emperor three years after the battle.

- He cleared the path for his descendants to continue the Tokugawa shogunate legacy until 1867-68.

- The Battle of Sekigahara put an end to the Warring States Period.

Two sets of daimyo were clearly discernible after the Battle of Sekigahara; the fudai and the tozama daimyo. The fudai were the ones who were loyal to the Tokugawa shogunate and the tozama were those who either opposed the Tokugawa or remained neutral.

The tozama were given increased lands while the fudai were given important political positions. The tozama were given more land to keep them happy giving them less reasons to rebel against the shogunate. The fudai were given powerful political posts to reward them for their loyalty. This clear distinction between the fudai and the tozama daimyo was visible right until the end of the Edo Period.

The Edo Period

The Tokugawa or the Edo shogunate was established by Tokugawa Ieyasu in 1603, and, therefore, this period between 1600 and 1867 is referred to as the Edo Period. During the Edo Period, Japan had very little or no influence from the outside world in terms of politics, religion or economically.

Only the Dutch East India Company and China had the right to visit Japan during the Edo Period. All other Europeans who landed on the shores of Japan were put to death. The Edo Period ended in 1867, when the last shogun, Tokugawa Yoshinobu, restored the imperial rule.

Economic Development during the Edo Period – The long period of peace during the Edo allowed for a lot of economic development to take place in Japan. There was increased urbanization, shipping of commodities, significant growth in domestic trade and commerce, and plenty of diffusion between trade and handicraft.

The population of Japan increased, and by the mid-18th century, Edo had a population of one million. In addition to the growth and development of urban centers like Kyoto and Osaka, smaller castle towns also flourished. Kyoto and Osaka were trading centers and handicrafts production centers. Edo was the center of food supplies and other essential urban consumer goods. Merchant associations, banking facilities and construction trades expanded. The daimyo authorities supervised the rural handicrafts and agricultural production.

Intellectual Progress during the Edo Period – Before the Tokugawa period, Confucianism was kept syncretized with Buddhism, and the Buddhist clerics kept Confucian studies alive. However, during the Edo period, Confucianism became free of Buddhism and its religious control.

Intellectual thoughts were more attuned to man and society than religion, God and spirituality. Rationalism and ethical humanitarianism of neo-Confucianism appealed to the official class in the Edo Period. By the mid-17th century, Confucianism was the country's dominant philosophy and it contributed to the growth and expansion of the kokugaku school of thought.

A deeper understanding of neo-Confucianism facilitated the transition of Japanese society from feudal system practices to class practices. New administrative devices and laws were promulgated. A new governing principle emerged that called for a comprehensive governance by the bakufu.

Every person in society had a distinct place and he or she was expected to work hard and fulfill his or her life's mission. The people assigned to rule had to do so with a benevolent attitude towards their subjects. The central government was very powerful but also humane and responsible. Clergy and soldiers were part of the ruling elite.

The samurai warriors renewed their vows to the bushido (the way of the warrior) code and learned from their history. A new way of life known as Chonindo emerged. Chonindo or the way of the townspeople was a new and distinct culture that grew and spread in cities such as Edo, Osaka and Kyoto. The Chonindo code encouraged the common people to rise up to bushido qualities such as honesty, diligence, frugality, honor and loyalty. It also blended humane qualities from Buddhist, Shinto, and Confucianism beliefs.

The Edo period rulers encouraged the study of astronomy, mathematics, medicine, cartography, and engineering. A lot of emphases was laid on the quality of workmanship, especially those involved in creating artworks. For the first time in the history of Japan, the urban population had the resources and time to create a mass culture of entertainment for themselves.

The search for entertainment by the urban populace of the Edo period was referred to as the ukiyo or the floating world which represented an ideal world of popular entertainment and fashion. This world of ukiyo had many entertainment elements including female entertainers or the geisha, popular stories, music, kabuki theater, bunraku (puppetry), rich literature and poetry and, finally, art in the form of beautiful woodblock prints called ukiyo-e.

Shinto and Buddhism were still important foundations of religion in the Edo Period. However, the emergence of neo-Confucianism helped set standards of social behavior. Christianity was not allowed to flourish and, in 1640, everyone in Japan had to register at a Buddhist temple, which favored the growth of Buddhism.

The society of Tokugawa was rigidly sectioned into households, wards, villages and han which helped in reaffirming local Shinto faith of each section and unit. Shinto offered spiritual support to the political order during the Edo period and was also an important connection between the community and individuals. Shinto helped in the preservation of a national identity in Japan.

Shinto took on an intellectual form when it was shaped by Confucianism thoughts of materialism and rationalism. The kokugaku movement was a combination of the beliefs of Confucianism and Shinto. Kokugaku facilitated the emergence of national pride centered upon the emperor and also helped in making Shinto a national creed in the 18th and 19th centuries.

The Nihon Shoki and the Kojiki were studied with renewed interest and with new perspectives. A few Shinto purists in the Kokugaku movement even criticized the influences of Buddhism and Confucianism on the original religion of Japan. They said these 'foreign' influences had corrupted the ancient pure ways of the Japanese people and culture. These purists believed that Japan was the land of the kami, and the island nation had a special destiny.

Western influences during the Edo period was almost completely restricted. There was a small school of thought called Rangaku or Dutch Learning whose adherents were restricted to Nagasaki which housed the Dutch outpost.

The Decline of the Tokugawa and the Arrival of the Americans

The decline of the Tokugawa shogunate is known as the 'Late Tokugawa Shogunate' and was rife with controversies. The primary reason for the fall of the Tokugawa shogunate was attributed to the forced opening of Japan to the outside world by the naval ships of Commodore Mathew Perry of the United States.

The Japanese people nicknamed Commodore Perry's Armada as 'the black ships.' These ships opened fire from Tokyo Bay forcing Japan to open its doors to foreigners which it had managed to keep out until now. The Japanese had created multiple land masses to block out the firing weapons from the armada. These blocks of land masses are located in present-day Obaida district.

While intrinsic failures contributed significantly to the collapse of the Tokugawa shogunate, there were other reasons as well. Foreign attacks precipitated existing complex political struggles between the shogunate and its critics. The anti-bakufu movement that continued into the mid-19th century was also a reason for its downfall.

Even from the start of their reign, the Tokugawa powers tried hard to restrict the accumulation of wealth by families. The shogunate, instead, fostered a 'back to the soil' policy wherein the farmer or the grower was the ideal individual in society. Despite the shogunate's attempts to restrict wealth accumulation, the standard of living in the whole of Japan (both urban and rural) went up considerably during the Edo Period.

The reasons for this increased standard of living were many including the long reign of peace, which allowed the people to focus on living better lives. Moreover, during this period, Japan witnessed a significant improvement in transportation, crop production, entertainment and the availability of food and clothing resulting in a happy, contented and luxurious life for all.

Literacy rates were high. There was a lot more leisure time than before which gave people an opportunity to redefine and implement new cultural values that were imparted impartially through the chonin and the samurai classes. Trade and commerce flourished beyond the restrictive barriers of guilds and a money-based economy developed.

The nobility did not really like the merchants and artisans because they had a perception of being usurious and unproductive. However, the samurai class depended on the merchant class to get them luxury consumer and artistic goods. Additionally, merchants gave loans to the samurai class when needed. Therefore, the chonin class subverted the warrior class slowly and subtly.

The government's policy of 'back to the soil' and giving farmers the ideal status did not go down well with the reality of trade and commerce. The restrictions laid on the entrepreneurial class made them restive and a struggle arose to break free from these governmental limitations.

Another important element that began to decay is the huge and now worthless bureaucracy, thanks to the changing and evolving social order. To add to these woes, the population in Japan increased in an unprecedented manner. As per a 1721 census, there were 26 million commoners, 4 million samurai members along with their entourage.

Twenty famines between 1675 and 1837 brought on by droughts and crop failures devastated Japan. Unrest among the peasant class increased and by the late 18th century, masses came out on the streets protesting about food shortages and taxes. Families who lost their land because of famines and other reasons became tenant farmers and the displaced poor from the rural areas migrated to the cities.

Previously wealthy families lost their wealth and new people moved in to take their place by accumulating land resulting in the emergence of a new class of wealthy farmers. The people who benefited from this period diversified their production and hired laborers. The ones who did not benefit were a discontented lot. Many of the samurais fell into really bad times and were forced to take up production of handicrafts or had to find jobs with merchants.

By the early 19th century, the western intrusions started to increase. Russian traders and warships landed and captured parts of Karafuto and Kuril islands, the northern parts of Hokkaido islands. A British warship came to Nagasaki scouting for Dutch enemy ships and many other foreign naval vessels were seen in Japanese territories. Trading ships and naval ships from the United States also landed on Japanese shores.

Barring a few trading concessions, the Japanese endeavored to keep foreign ships out as much as possible. Sometimes, they even resorted to force for this purpose. The Rangaku school of thought became an important subject now because it helped them understand foreign languages, thought, and philosophy, which the Japanese used to fend off the foreigners who tried to land in their country.

By the 1830s, a sense of crisis was prevalent throughout the country. Badly affected by natural disasters, the restless peasants revolted against the merchants and government officials in 1837 in Osaka. The uprising lasted only one day. But the government swung into action. They brought about reforms targeted at reforming decay. They did nothing to address institutional and administrative problems.

Some of the shogunate's advisors urged for policies that would bring back the martial spirit with even more restrictions on foreign contact and trade. They wanted to suppress the Rangaku, censor art and literature and bring back the earlier frugal lifestyle. The luxurious lifestyle of the samurai class had to be abolished.

Some other advisors wanted to overthrow the Tokugawa shogunate called for sonno-joi, a political doctrine to 'revere the emperor and expel the barbarian.' This doctrine called for unity of the country under imperial rule and opposed all foreign intrusions. For the time being, the bakufu persevered amidst all the restlessness and strife. There was a growing concern of foreign threats even as news about colonization in China reached Japan. More reforms with special emphasis on economics and trade were promulgated to prevent the encroachment of foreigners on Japanese soil.

In July 1846, Commodore James Biddle landed in Edo Bay in a bid to set up US diplomatic relations in Japan. He brought with him two warships. However, the Japanese turned down this offer of diplomacy from the US, which was on its own path to spread its influence in the Asia-Pacific region.

In July 1853, a four-ship squadron under the command of Commodore Matthew C. Perry landed in Edo Bay. Now, the bakufu was in a turmoil. Abe Masahiro, the chairman of the bakufu's senior councilors, was in charge of talking to the Americans. With no prior experience in handling such national security situations, Abe Masahiro attempted to balance the following elements:

- The senior councilors wanted to compromise with the Americans

- The emperor wanted to keep the Americans out

- The daimyo wanted to declare war on them

There was no consensus reached, and therefore, Abe Masahiro compromised by accepting Perry's demand for opening trade routes and also preparing the military for war. In March 1854, the Treaty of Kanagawa (or the Treaty of Peace and Amity) was signed which benefited the Americans in the following ways:

- Two ports were opened for American ships to land and carry on trade

- Shipwrecked American sailors had to be given good treatment

- A US consul was allowed to set up residence in Shimoda, a seaport located southwest of Edo, in the Izu Peninsula

Five years later in 1859, the Americans forced the Japanese to open more areas for trade. The bakufu was the worst hit because of all these events. It got a lot of public criticism thanks to the various unusual debates taking place about governance and government policies.

To make matters worse, Abe Masahiro consulted the tozama daimyo in all the discussions, which angered and created resentment in the bakufu in addition to undermining the authority of the already weak bakufu. Abe then tried to re-strengthen bakufu power by:

- Ordering Dutch armaments and warships
- Building new defenses at the ports
- Opening a naval school at Nagasaki in 1955 with Dutch instructors
- Setting up a Western-style army school in Edo
- Translating western books into Japanese

Despite all these attempts, resentment against Abe increased within the fudai daimyo set because he opened the gates of the council to the tozama daimyo. In 1855, Hotta Masayoshi replaced him as the chairman of the senior councilors of the bakufu.

Tokugawa Nariaki was one of the most important dissident factions. He embraced a militant-type loyalty to the emperor and wanted to drive out the foreigners. He was in charge of national defense. The primary goal of The Mito School, which was founded on Shinto and Confucianism beliefs was to restore the power of the emperor, throw out the western influences, and establish a world empire under the Yamato Dynasty.

Towards the end of the Tokugawa rule, foreign contracts increased as more and more ports were thrown open to the Americans. Unsupervised trade at four additional ports was also allowed. Foreign residences were opened in Edo and Osaka. These foreigners also got the advantage of extraterritoriality which meant the Americans were guided by their own laws even in Japan and were not covered by Japanese laws.

Hotta sought imperial sanction when Tokugawa Nariaki opposed the treaty. Now, seeing the weakening power of the bakufu, the imperial court rejected its plea, and for the first time in many centuries, the emperor was embroiled in Japan's internal political strife.

When the shogun died without leaving an heir, Tokugawa Nariaki requested the imperial court's support to place his own son, Tokugawa Yoshinobu, as shogun. This candidate had the support of the tozama and shinpan (certain relatives of the Tokugawa clan) daimyo. However, the fudai daimyo emerged victorious in this power struggle and had Tokugawa Yoshitomi installed as the shogun and arrested Nariaki and Yoshinobu (or Keiki).

Yoshida Shoin, an important sonno-joi proponent who had vehemently opposed compromise with the Americans, was executed too. These events brought an end to Japanese exclusion from the outside world.

However, these strong measures of the bakufu to regain its lost authority were insufficient. Extremists loyal to Japanese imperialism wreaked havoc on foreigners, the bakufu, and the Han (bakufu-appointed administrative posts) authorities. Another foreign naval attack forced the signing of a new commercial treaty in 1865. But, the bakufu could not enforce this treaty. A bakufu army was defeated when it tried to crush a rebellion led by Choshu and Satsuma daimyo.

In 1867, when the emperor died, his minor son, Mitsuhito, succeeded him, and Keiki was made shogun and head of the Tokugawa family. Keiki tried to bring order to the government while maintaining the supremacy of his clan. Fearing the growing strength of the Choshu and Satsuma daimyo, the others called for restoring the power to the emperor under the advice of the council of daimyo. Keiki was to become the chairman of this council, and in 1867, this plan was put into action.

However, the Choshu and Satsuma along with other rebelling daimyo, revolted and captured the imperial palace in 1868. The bakufu was abolished with Keiki being reduced to a commoner daimyo. And, that ended the shogunate in Japan.

Chapter 4: Modern Japan

The modern history of Japan can be divided into:

- The Meiji Restoration (1868 – 1912 CE)
- The Taisho Period (1912 – 1926 CE)

The Meiji Restoration

The start of the Meiji Restoration coincided with the end of the shogunate era and feudalism in Japan. This period is also characteristic of modernization and westernization of Japan. The country reached a status of world power during the Meiji Era. The period starts with, Mutsuhito, the minor son of Emperor Komei, ascending the Kyoto throne in 1867. He took on the title of Meiji meaning 'enlightened rule.'

Mutsuhito, Emperor of Japan

The Charter of Oath of 1868 was the first step that Emperor Meiji to set the nation on the course of modernization. This important charter consisted of five articles:

1. Extensive public discussions will determine government plans and policies. These discussions will take place through established assemblies

2. All classes of society will work together to realize government plans.

3. Discrimination among classes of society will not be there and everyone will be free to achieve their aspirations; class distinctions should not prevent people from trying to achieve their dreams

4. New rules and regulations based on the laws of nature will replace old, evil practices

5. Knowledge will be sought and gained from all over the world to strengthen the power of Japanese imperial rule

The Meiji Period was a remarkable period in the history of Japan because it rose to a global power status in an exceedingly short time. There are primarily two reasons for this almost miraculously growth in Japan:

1. Over 3000 foreign experts were hired to help in the modernization and westernization process. These experts, referred to as o-yatoi gaikokujin (hired foreigners), worked in a variety of areas including English language teaching, engineering, science, defense, and more.

2. Many Japanese students were sent to America and Europe to learn skills associated with modern advanced technologies and to return home so that they could

implement their learning to make Japan modern and efficient

The process of sending students abroad and employing foreign experts and then converting the expertise to tangible results was closely monitored by the Meiji government. The subsidies needed for these processes were provided by large zaibatsus (Japanese conglomerates) such as Mitsubishi and Mitsui.

Thanks to the modernization and industrialization, Japan controlled a large percentage of Asian manufacturing markets. The Japanese economy worked like a merchant trading company. It purchased raw materials from one source, converted it into finished goods in their factories, which were then exported to other countries.

The biggest disadvantage for Japan was the fact that it lacked raw materials and it had to depend on other resource-rich countries for it, which was the reason for a trader-like approach taken by the Meiji government.

In order to keep control over resource-rich regions, Japan indulged in and won many strategic wars during the Meiji Era. It defeated China in the Sino-Japanese War of 1894-1895 resulting in the control over mining land. It defeated Russia in the Russo-Japanese war in Manchuria in 1904-1905. The fact that Japan was allied with Britain since the

Anglo-Japanese alliance signed in 1902 in London helped its cause.

Under the guise of WWI battles, Japan captured many German-occupied territories in the Pacific and China. Otherwise, Japan remained outside the influences of WWI conflicts. It chose only to leverage benefits of the war to gain control over regions that provided raw materials for its industrial purposes. Therefore, when the war ended, Europe had become very weak but Japan emerged strong and powerful. Moreover, a larger percentage of the world markets was available to Japan than before the war.

Itagaki Taisuke

Representative Government

The people of Japan were introduced to the concept of a representative form of government during the Meiji Period. Itagaki Taisuke, a very powerful Tosa leader, was a strong contender of this issue.

Itagaki used peaceful means instead of violent ways to include the common man's voices in government formation. His Tosa Memorial of 1874 criticized the oligarchy and called for an immediate setting up of a representative government. Itagaki organized all his supporters and other people who wanted democracy into a national society called Aikokusha or the Society of Patriots in 1878. In 1881, Itagaki was one of the founding members of Jiyuto or the Liberal Party.

In 1882, Okuma Shigenobu pushed for a British-style democratic government. Okuma founded Constitutional Progressive Party or the Rikken Kaishinto. Additionally, government officials, bureaucrats, and other conservative Japanese formed the Imperial Rule Party or the Rikken Teiseito in the same year.

There were multiple political demonstrations calling for a representative form of government including some violent ones. These demonstrations that hampered the aims of the Meiji government forced it to bring in some policy-making restrictions.

These government restrictions hindered the operations of the political parties so much so that internal strife and divisions reared their ugly heads within each of them. The Jiyuto was disbanded in 1884, and Okuma resigned as the leader of the Kaishinto Party.

Although many government leaders believed that a representational form of government would one day be the norm in Japan and although the imperial court acknowledged the truth of these political pressures, they did little to make big changes. They were also determined to maintain their control over the government.

Consequently, during the Meiji Period, a few nominal changes (like the following) were allowed through the 1875 Osaka conference:

- Reorganization of the Meiji government

- An independent judiciary

- An appointed Council of Elders or Genronin

The emperor declared the constitutional form of government would be established gradually. The Genronin was tasked with drafting the constitution. After a few years, elected assemblies were formed at the prefecture, village and town levels. Although these assemblies had very limited powers, it was a definite step toward a democratic setup reaching the national level.

In 1880, the League for Establishing a National Assembly or Kokkai Kisei Domei was set up by the representatives of 24 prefectures. The Meiji regime did not openly oppose the parliamentary type of government but it did not give up trying to control the political situation in Japan.

For example, in 1875, any kind of criticism by the press against the government was banned. Discussions of national laws in press media was banned. Organizing public gatherings was made more difficult by introducing mandatory requirements for prior police permissions. Civil servants were also not allowed to attend these gatherings.

Despite all these pressures, Okuma continued his fight for a British-styled representative form of government. He vehemently called for elections in 1882. His diligence did have some payoff because an 1881 imperial rescript declared that a national assembly would be set up in 1890. It was a big positive step even if the pace of the progress was much slower than Okuma's expectations.

Drafting the Japanese Constitution

The British model proposed by Okuma was rejected. Instead, the Prussian constitutional system was taken up for study and replication in Japan. Ito Hirobumi, a trusted member of the Meiji oligarchy and with many years of experience in managing government affairs was given the responsibility to draft the constitution of Japan. He went abroad on a study tour.

- He rejected the US Constitution for being excessively liberal

- He rejected the British Constitution for being excessive unwieldy and for having undue controls over the monarchy

- The Spanish and French models were rejected for leaning toward despotism

When Ito returned from his Study Mission, one of the first changes to take place was to set up new ranks among the nobility in the Meiji oligarchy. Former daimyo, samurai, and over 500 old-court nobles were divided into five ranks including:

1. Prince
2. Marquis
3. Count

4. Viscount

5. Baron

A new Bureau for Investigation of Constitutional Systems was set up in 1884, and Ito was put in charge of this committee. In 1885, the Council of State was abolished and was replaced by a cabinet with Ito being its prime minister. The earlier positions of advisors to the emperor which were in existence from the 7th century were all abolished. These included the minister of left, the minister of right, the chancellor, etc. In their place, a Privy Council was set up in 1888 as an advisory council for the emperor. The first job of this Privy Council was to evaluate the upcoming constitution of Japan.

Further, a Supreme War Council was established headed by Yamagata Aritomo who later went on to become the first constitutional prime minister in the country. He is also credited with setting up the modern Japanese army. The Supreme War Council had a chief of staff who could directly report to the emperor and could act independently of the civilian minister and the army minister.

The Meiji Constitution or the Constitution of the Empire of Japan was finally signed off by the emperor and promulgated in 1889. This constitution provided for the Teikoku Gikai or the Imperial Diet consisting of an elected House of Representatives and the House of Peers, which had imperial appointees and people from nobility as members. The Constitution also provided for a cabinet independent of the legislature and reported directly to the emperor.

The Diet could initiate laws and approve legislation. It could make representations to the government as well as submit petitions to the imperial court. However, despite all these constitutional elements coming into play in Japan, the emperor continued to be the sovereign leader with divine ancestry.

The Meiji Constitution still only provided for an authoritarian government with the emperor having the ultimate power with minimal concessions given to parliamentary mechanisms and popular rights and benefits for the common man. The Meiji Constitution was in force until 1947.

The weaknesses and strengths of the Meiji Constitution were revealed in the initial stages. Some of the Choshu and Satsuma elite became institutionalized as the genro or the body of elders, an extraconstitutional segment of the government. This body took decisions that were typically reserved for the emperor. And it was the genro and not the emperor that effectively ruled over Japan.

Right through the Meiji period, the political parties slowly started to gain power and actively participated in the political process of the government. All political problems were typically solved through compromise. Ito was the prime minister between 1891 and 1895 and had a cabinet consisting mostly of the genro who aimed at creating a government party to control the House of Representatives.

Modernization of Japan

Apart from all these political changes, the Meiji period is more associated with the emergence of Japan as an industrialized nation. Right from the beginning, the Meiji rulers had preferred the North American and British styled free market economy and capitalism. The nation which had an abundant supply of aggressive entrepreneurs welcomed this change.

Important economic reforms of the Meiji Era included:

- A unified modern currency
- Tax, commercial and banking laws
- A communications network
- Stock exchanges

The Meiji government did not hesitate to set up a political and institutional framework that was conducive to a highly advanced capitalized economy. Yes, the process took some time. But, by the 1890s, the much-needed work on the capitalism-based political and economic changes was in place. Moreover, by the 1890s, the government relinquished its direct control of the modernization process mostly for budgetary reasons. The zaibatsus took over this task on their own.

Many of the erstwhile daimyos who got pensions in lumpsum benefited greatly from the investments they made in the modernization process. Those who informally were into foreign investments even before the Meiji Restoration also benefited significantly. The only ones who failed were the ones who chose to cling on to the old bakufu traditions and conventions.

During the initial period of modernization, the Meiji government set up multiple model factories to help in the transition process. After the first 20 years, the industrialization process expanded rapidly using western technology and helped by large private investments. Cautious economic planning and with some help from the aftermath of war Japan emerged as a global industrial power after WWI.

Emperor Meiji died in 1912 after which Emperor Taisho ascended the throne and started the Taisho Era.

The Taisho Era

Emperor Taisho was not a very powerful ruler, which resulted in the shift of government authority from imperialism to democracy. The Taisho Era, also known as the 'Taisho Democracy,' is characterized by the transfer of power from the genro to the parliament.

The Meiji Legacy

Although a lot of modernization and industrialization took place during the Meiji Restoration, the domestic situation was not as perfect as it seemed. Government credit and foreign exchange were down.

Another effect of the Meiji Restoration was peasant unrest. During the initial years, the Meiji Government directly invested in setting up factories. The resources for the establishment of these factories came from high taxes, and the peasant class provided exploitative cheap labor.

Once the factory started making profits, it was sold off to capitalists (zaibatsus). The coffers of the Meiji government filled and the capitalists were happy too. However, the peasant class was badly hit and they rebelled against the injustice even during the Meiji Era, which continued into the Taisho Era.

The leftist movements failed too despite their noble intentions. The early socialist movements of Japan fought for social welfare, universal male suffrage and workers' rights. They undertook nonviolent protests to voice these demands. The Meiji government did everything in its power to suppress the leftist movements and were able to wind up the activities of the Japan Socialist Party.

Although the socialist movement failed during the Meiji Era, they were able to instill a sense of fair play and justice among the people of Japan who continued to raise demands for equality and voice their protests against exploitation. These movements continued into the Taisho Era

World War I

The Taisho Era witnessed an increased expansionist attitude. Germany had territorial control in China at that time. Now, Germany was distracted by its wars in Europe. Japan seized this opportunity and expanded its territories in China by attacking and capturing some German-controlled areas included Inner Mongolia, Manchuria and Shangdong Province. Japan also got control of many islands in the Pacific including Marshall, Mariana and Caroline islands.

In 1915, encouraged by their successes so far and with the intention of strengthening its position in China, Japan presented a list of 21 demands including joint ownership in mining rights in resource-rich Chinese areas, a ban on China to lease out coastal areas to third parties, and multiple other controls. These demands, if given, would have threatened the sovereignty of China.

But, fortunately for China, Japan itself withdrew many of its excessive demands from that list of 21. The reasons for withdrawal were:

- The negotiations were progressing at a very slow pace

- Anti-Japanese sentiments were spreading wide and fast among the Chinese people, and the Japanese government was acutely aware of this unpleasant sentiments

In May 1915, after Japan withdrew the excessive conditions from the list of demands, the peace negotiations were settled between the two countries. This negotiation settlement with and territorial domination over China helped Japan get other international agreements completed too.

For example, in 1916, A Russo-Japanese agreement secured Japan's control over parts of Sakhalin Islands and Manchuria, the Liaodong Peninsula including the strategically located Port Arthur, and the South Manchurian Railway. Additionally, Japan signed agreements with the US, France and Britain, which recognized its control and annexure of captured territories in China and the Pacific islands.

Japan had extended loans (referred to as Nishihara loans) to China in 1917-1918, which put China in further debt of the Japanese government. As World War I progressed, especially toward the end, Japan got a lot of orders for war materials from many European countries, which resulted in increased export earnings. All these events during WWI helped Japan transform itself from being a nation in debt to being a nation in credit.

The end of the tsarist regime in Russia and the Bolshevik Revolutions threw the country into chaos. This situation was also favorable for Japan as it increased its opportunities to become a nation of power and prestige in East Asia.

Moreover, the Japanese navy captured German-controlled Micronesian colonies.

The following events in Japan between 1916 and 1918 affected its politics and society in many ways:

- Terauchi Masatake became prime minister after Okuma in 1916

- The Lansing-Ishii agreement with the US recognized Japan's control and interest in China

- In July 1918, Japan sent 75,000 of its troops as part of the Allied nations army to attack and capture Siberia; this will be one of the reasons for the economic drain in the country later on

- And, finally, in August 1918, cities and towns of Japan erupted in what is now famously known as rice riots precipitated by many issues including the increasing costs of rice and peasant unrest carried forward from the Meiji Restoration period. These riots caused the downfall of Terauchi Masatake's administration.

Japan after WWI

When the war ended, Japan emerged as an important global player. At the Versailles Peace Conference, Japan was one of the 'Big Five' countries of the world along with Great Britain, the US, Italy and France. Japan was offered a permanent seat on the League of Nations Council. This was the beginning of an era of unprecedented peace and prosperity for Japan, which lasted until halfway through WWII.

Thanks to multiple domestic issues including peasant unrest, which culminated in the Rice Riots of August 1918, Terauchi Masatake's administration fell. Hara Takashi, a commoner became the prime minister. He used several tried and tested political methods to maintain his majority.

His administration promulgated new electoral laws, electoral arrangements were redistribution, and numerous public works funded by the government were launched; all done to keep as many people as happy as possible so that he could keep the majority.

However, public disillusionment and resent did not end. The new electoral laws had very little changes. Even in this new set of laws, the old system of giving voting benefits only to a certain section of tax-paying citizens continued. Universal male suffrage was not yet in place.

Therefore, public protests went on right through 1919 and 1920. Everyone in the society participating in these nonviolent protests. University professors, students, labor unions, journalists and other large and influential groups in society actively participated in these protests. The people of Japan wanted the old political system completely disbanded as well as universal male suffrage to be implemented.

Hara was assassinated in 1921 in the midst of all these protests and upheavals. He was shot at by a disgruntled railroad employee. Now, the government in power, the Seiyokai Party, was worried that a wider electorate, increasing calls for social changes, and the rising power of communism would damage their chances to retain power. To counter all these situations, the government passed a new policy called the Peace Preservation Law in 1925.

This rather draconian law forbade any social changes from taking place. It also prevented the abolishment of private property, a critical element in the leftist movement agenda. Despite these measures, domestic economic crises continued to put the Seiyokai Party on the defensive.

Interestingly, the Great Depression of the 1930s did not impact Japan. In fact, the country's exports grew significantly. But, discontent among the locals continued to increase.

Communism in Japan

The Bolshevik Revolution in 1917 in Russia raised the hopes of communists to achieve world recognition. The Comintern was set up in Moscow in 1919 which intended to take Communism to the world. The Comintern was acutely aware of the strategic importance of Japan for their purpose. Therefore, the Comintern actively helped the Japanese left-wingers to set up the Japan Communist Party in July 1922.

The goals of the Japan Communist Party included:

- To end feudalism

- To abolish the monarchy system of governance in Japan

- To get recognition for the Soviet Union

- To get Japan to withdraw its troops from Siberia and other occupied places.

However, all these were easier said than done. The party was brutally suppressed. In fact, the Peace Preservation Law of 1925 was the government's way of retaliating against increasing threats from communism. Moreover, the police department worked very efficiently and their networking and operational efficiency helped the government control and suppress leftists' agenda.

The Japan Communist Party was banned. By 1926, its leaders went underground, and by 1929, many of its prominent leadership were imprisoned or killed. By 1933, the leftist symbol in the country, the Japan Communist Party, was totally annihilated.

Another element that worked against communism in Japan were the ultra-nationalist societies set up by erstwhile samurai warriors. Right from the beginning of the Meiji Restoration period, ultra-nationalism was a primary agenda of conservative politicians and military men.

With the help of these right-wing leaders, former samurai warriors established patriotic societies that did a lot of undercover and intelligence work for the government. These societies also spread pro-war sentiments among the public. They remained active until the end of WWII and contributed significantly to the downfall of the leftist movement in Japan.

Foreign Policy

For a long time, Japan dominated the politics of East Asia, thanks to its growing economy and its increasing control over multiple dominions, and despite internal domestic discontentment. However, some things changed during the 1920s. Communism was gaining popularity in China and other Asian countries. Nationalism was gaining ground in China. The US was expanding its footprints across East Asia.

All these elements worked against the prevailing belligerence of Japan's foreign policy. Moreover, the protracted Siberian expedition drain its coffers. Increased spending within the country was eating into the hefty earnings made during WWI.

Japan realized that to remain a dominant player in East Asia, it must increase its business competitiveness, which, in turn, would lead to an improved economy and coffers refilling again. They could not antagonize the US because it was the primary source of raw materials. The events in China were also affecting Japan's foreign policy.

Therefore, Japan decided to tone down its military aggression for some time. It gave up its expansion schemes in China. It took a neutral stand in the Civil War in China. Like France, Britain and the US, Japan too took an ostensible stand of promoting China's self-development plans. By 1922,

Japan withdrew all its troops from Chinese territories including the Shandong province and Siberia as well.

End of the Taisho Era

During the 1920s, Japan made steady progress towards a democratic form of society. However, the parliamentary principles were still not deeply rooted to withstand political and economic pressures of the 1930s. The military rulers in Japan grew increasingly influential during the 1930s.

This kind of power shifting between democracy and imperialism was possible because of the tenuous and ambiguous nature of the Meiji Constitution, especially with regard to the stand of the emperor and the imperial court. The Meiji Constitution spared no words to put the emperor above everyone else. He was sacred, divine and heaven-sent. He is inviolable and must be respected.

Finally, in December 1926, Emperor Taisho died, and his successor, Emperor Hirohito, became emperor of Japan.

Chapter 5: Contemporary Japan

For ease of understanding and to keep the flow of thoughts in an unbroken chain, this book divides contemporary Japan into the following historical periods:

- The Showa Period (1926 – 1989 CE)
- The Heisei Period (1989 – present day)

The Showa Period

Emperor Hirohito ruled over Japan during the Showa Period. He ruled from December 25, 1926, until January 7, 1989, and is the longest-serving emperor of Japan. The early part of his rule was imperialistic in nature and after the post-WWII surrender, his rule was predominantly in a democratic setting. The Showa Period can be subdivided into the following:

- Expansionism (1926 – 1945)
- The American Occupation (1945 – 1952)
- Post-Occupation Japan (1952 – 1989)

Expansionism

After the Great Depression, like many other countries, Japan also followed fascism, although it was a unique form as compared to the ones followed in Germany (Adolf Hitler) and Italy (Benito Mussolini). Despite the uniqueness of fascism in Japan (probably because of the cultural differences), it was similar to the European form in many ways just like how Japanese feudalism was similar to European feudalism.

However, Japan had two very clear and primary goals in establishing a fascist empire. The first reason was that a well-controlled military-based industry would give an amazing jumpstart to the country's economy. Second, Japan lacked raw materials and had to depend on other countries such as Taiwan, China, the US, and Korea for raw materials such as iron, coal, oil, etc.

While most of the raw materials came from the US, Japan took on an expansionist attitude of annexing colonies to get raw materials it lacked in its homeland. Formosa (present-day Taiwan) and Korea were annexed in 1895 and 1910 respectively primarily for their agricultural resources. Manchuria was needed for its iron and coal, Indochina for rubber, and China's vast and rich resources for multiple other raw materials.

Japan attacked and captured Manchuria in 1931 with no resistance. For ostensible reasons, Japan's attack on

Manchuria was to free it from China just like how it called its attack on Korea in 1910 as an act of protection. A puppet government was set up in Manchuria while Japan controlled it from Kyoto. Jehol, another Chinese territory bordering Manchuria was annexed in 1933.

In 1937, Japan attacked China and set off a three-way war where the stakeholders were Japan, the communists of Mao Zedong, and the nationalists of Chiang Kai-shek. While Japan carefully avoided the European-controlled regions in China, it slowly but surely took control of much of China's port cities and coastal areas. Japan had signed an anti-communist treaty with Germany and Italy before it invaded China.

In 1937, Japan and China went into full-fledged war, the Second Sino-Japanese War which didn't end as well as the First Sino-Japanese War ended for Japan. This time around, the nationalists in China did not give up very easily and the war became a protracted one pushing Japan and its economy to the brink.

Supplies of oil, rubber, and iron had its breaking point, and to make matters worse, Japan had no allies in the region. It had antagonized nearly all the nations in East Asia. The world began to view Japan as a rogue state. Japan was in a confused state. The reason for its militarization and industrialization was to increase economic growth as well as be seen as an international power. Both were not happening at this time.

In a desperate bid to get raw materials needed to get its factories going, Japan attacked Malaya, the Philippines, Hong Kong, Singapore, and Pearl Harbor simultaneously. These attacks turned out to be suicidal for Japan as they did not foresee the reaction of the US for the Pearl Harbor. The US aiming atom bombs at Nagasaki and Hiroshima was the ultimate blow to Japan and they surrendered on August 14, 1945.

The American Occupation

When Emperor Hirohito surrendered in 1945, he accepted the terms of the Potsdam Declaration. It was the end of WWII and the beginning of a long and arduous journey of recovery from its shattering defeat for Japan.

At Potsdam, Harry Truman (US President) and Josef Stalin (the premiere of the USSR) had agreed on how the Allied occupation will be carried out. The Soviet Union was to be responsible for Kuril islands, Korea and Sakhalin, and the US was to manage Japan and its remaining territories in Oceania and South Korea.

President Truman appointed General Douglas MacArthur as Supreme Commander of the Allied Powers (SCAP) in-charge of Japanese occupation. Sixteen Japanese were sent to Manila on August 19th, 1945, for a meeting with the General to hear his plans on the Occupation. On August 28th, 1945, 150 American personnel and staff flew to Atsugi in Kanagawa Prefecture to start work on the American Occupation of Japan. These 150 Americans were followed by the US Naval Ship, the USS Missouri which brought the Fourth Marines to the southern coast of Kanagawa.

General MacArthur landed in Tokyo on August 30th. He immediately set forth certain rules for his men:

- No American was to fraternize with Japanese women

- No American was allowed to strike any Japanese man
- No American was allowed to consume Japanese food

Japan formally surrendered on September 2nd when they signed the Japanese Instrument of Surrender, and the Occupation formally began on this day. General MacArthur's first task was to establish a food distribution network because after the devastation of the war, and wholesale destruction of cities, villages and towns, nearly everyone was starving.

When the food network was set in place, General MacArthur went about trying to win the approval of Emperor Hirohito. The two of them met on September 28, and their photograph together is, perhaps, one of the most important memorabilia of Japanese history. After obtaining the emperor's sanction, General MacArthur went about the work of Occupation.

Accomplishments of General MacArthur

Disarmament – One of the first tasks that the General undertook after landing in Japan was to ask all Japanese personnel to give up their daito (long sword) and (short swords) shoto. Several tons of swords were collected and shipped off to San Francisco. The police force was completely disbanded and a new 'Peace' clause was added to the constitution, which forbade the Japanese government from waging war.

Liberalization – The country's zaibatsu, the large conglomerates that were partly responsible for the modernization of Japan during the Meiji Restoration, were all dismantled with only the factories remaining intact. Over 20,000 km² of land was confiscated from the nobles and handed over to the farmers who were working on the land.

Democratization – In 1946, General MacArthur established a new US-styled constitution which was ratified not as a new constitution but an amendment of the Meiji Constitution. The most important elements of these constitutional amendments included:

- Basic civil liberties and freedom rights guaranteed to all Japanese citizens

- Abolishment of all types of nobility

- The emperor was now the 'spiritual leader' of the country and all his political powers were vested from him

- Abolishment of Shinto as a state religion and acceptance of a Christianity as another religion available for the people to follow if they chose

- Female suffrage came into effect resulting in 14 million of them turning out to vote prime minister Yoshida Shigeru into power in April 1946

Unionization – Communism was, perhaps, one of the biggest challenges for General MacArthur. The communist feeling was brewing underground for some time now and was waiting for an opportunity to return. The Occupation's liberal environment gave communism the needed impetus. In February 1947, workers all over Japan called for a general strike.

General MacArthur sternly warned the workers with dire consequences if they went ahead with the strike. The unions finally relented resulting in a loss of face which effectively kept them quiet for the rest of the Occupation.

Education reforms – Before the Occupation, Japan followed the German-styled education system with universities and gymnasiums to train children after their primary school. General MacArthur abolished this system and brought in a US-styled education system which consisted of 3-year junior schools followed by senior school years. Attending and completing junior high school was compulsory whereas senior high school was optional.

The Imperial University system was changed and the Imperial Rescript on Education was repealed. Written Japanese was altered considerably and grammar was changed to align with conversational use.

War leaders were purged – While all these education, social, and political reforms were taking place in Japan, Japanese war leaders were being tried through various military tribunals. The most famous tribunal was the International Military Tribunal for the Far East in Ichigaya. War criminals were sentenced to imprisonment and death. When these old-school war leaders were completely purged, a new set of young leaders were trained to take on the mantle of the country.

The End of Occupation

In 1949, after doing completing his work, General Douglas MacArthur made sweeping changes to the SCAP powers that significantly increased the power and authority of the native rulers. This change in attitude was primarily because the US's attention was turned to the Korean War, and General MacArthur was needed there.

The Occupation of Japan ended formally with the San Francisco Peace Treaty of 1951 and when this treaty came into effect on April 28, 1952, Japan once again became an independent country.

Post-Occupation Japan

When the Allied Occupation of Japan ended in 1952, Japan emerged as a world economic power that surpassed its military powers of the pre-war days.

Politics and Economy in Post-Occupation Japan – As per the terms of the Treaty of San Francisco, Japan regained its sovereignty on April 28, 1952. However, the country lost some of its pre-war territories including the Kuril Islands, Okinawa, Sakhalin, and many other smaller islands in the Pacific. The new treaty allowed Japan to build its own global defense blocs. Additionally, the US Armed Forces were allowed to continue to keep their Japanese bases.

In 1955, the Liberal Democratic Party (LPD), a newly-formed political party, won a majority and remained in power unchallenged right up until 1990. The LDP government allowed development of Japanese industries overseas but restricted overseas businesses within the country. These practices along with its defense being managed by the US Armed Forces ensured that Japan prospered during the Cold War era.

By 1980, many of Japanese products and consumer goods particularly electronics and automobiles were exported all over the globe. Japan's industrial sector was the second-biggest in the world after the US. This unprecedented growth pattern continued until the 1990s when the economy of Japan again began to decline.

The 1964 Summer Olympics in Japan was an event that showcased Japan's amazing growth story to the world. The country's post-war re-emergence into the world arena was showcased through various innovations including the Shinkansen high-speed rail network.

The Yoshida Doctrine – After Yoshida Shigeru came to power in after the US occupation, he promulgated the Yoshida Doctrine which contained a policy that facilitated the growth and re-emergence of the country as a world economic power. The Doctrine allowed the country's resources to be used for economic production with the support of well-trained workers.

Yoshida decided to adopt the US stance on international politics and security matters. This doctrine led to the amazing economic growth of Japan and was the country's guiding principle regarding foreign and economic policies for decades after its promulgation.

The Culture in Post-Occupation Japan – During the post-occupation era, the westernization of Japanese culture continued. American movies and music were introduced into Japan during the Occupation and caught the imagination of many Japanese artists who built a new culture that combined the western and their own influences.

Post-occupation Japan was a period when Japanese culture was being exported all over the world, particularly to the US. The global audience was consuming anime (cartoons), kanji (monster movies), manga (comics), and other cultural aspects of Japan. American soldiers returning home after the Occupation carried with them stories, legends and artifacts from Japan that intrigued the Americans.

Japanese authors such as Yukio Mishima and Yasunari Kawabata were very popular in Europe and the US. Japanese filmmakers like Akira Kurosawa created waves in Hollywood.

Emperor Hirohito

When Emperor Hirohito took over the reins of Japan in 1926, the country was undergoing a democratization process though at a slow pace. Very soon, Japan turned to militarism and ultra-nationalism under his rule. Before WWII, Japan attacked and annexed many of its neighboring Asian countries and allied itself with Nazi Germany during WWII. Japan attacked the US base Pearl Harbor which was the beginning of the end of Japan's militarism.

Although Emperor Hirohito presented a picture of being a powerless emperor during WWII, most historians believe that he played a major role in making critical war-related decisions in Japan. After Japan surrendered in 1945, he became a 'spiritual leader' and only a constitutional head with no political powers.

His Early Years – Hirohito was born in 1901 in Aoyama Palace in Tokyo. As per Japanese tradition, he was not brought up under his parent's care but a retired vice-admiral first followed by an imperial attendant. He attended various schools set up for nobility and received rigorous training in religious and military matters. He also learned modern subjects such as science and math. In the year 1921, Hirohito along with a 34-member entourage went on a 6-month tour of Western Europe. This was the first time in the history of Japanese history when a crown prince left the shores of the country.

By the time he returned from his tour, Hirohito's father had become chronically ill, and he was appointed the regent. In September 1923, a devastating earthquake hit Tokyo killing over 100,000 people and leaving behind a trail of destruction. Japanese mobs went on a rampage killing thousands of Koreans, other foreigners and leftists after a rumor that they were responsible for looting and plundering Japanese homes.

Hirohito married Princess Nagako and they had seven children over several years of marriage. Hirohito ended the age-old and accepted practice of imperial concubinage in Japan and when he became emperor after his father's death in 1926, he took on the name of Showa for his period of rule.

Hirohito as Emperor of Japan – When Hirohito ascended the throne, pro-democracy was at its pre-war peak. However, many elements including rising militarism, declining economy, and numerous political assassinations stemmed the growth of democracy in Japan. Emperor Hirohito fired the prime minister in 1929 while the next candidate was shot at and assassinated by naval officers because they were upset with a government policy that restricted Japanese warships.

The prime ministers after this incident were all from the military rather than political parties, which were anyway completely disbanded in 1940. In 1935, a lot more political disturbances took place when a lieutenant colonel killed a general with a samurai sword. In 1936, over 1400 soldiers revolted in Tokyo. They killed many high-ranking politicians and seized the army ministry.

Meanwhile, conflict with China was rising and, in 1931, after setting a bomb on the railroad in Manchuria, which they blamed on some bandits, Japan attacked and captured Manchuria under the guise of protecting it. A puppet government, Manchukuo was set up there. More such military excursions followed, and by 1937, war broke out between Japan and China.

While Hirohito did not sanction nor condone the atrocities committed by the soldiers of the Japanese armies in the conquered territories, his fear of getting abdicated prevented him from punishing the perpetrators. Moreover, he approved chemical warfare and allowed peasants to be uprooted.

Emperor Hirohito and WWII – In September 1940, Japan signed a Tripartite Treaty with Italy and Germany to help each other during WWII. Japan sent its army to capture French-occupied Indochina and the US reacted to this by serving economic sanctions including an embargo on steel and iron.

In 1941, Emperor Hirohito approved his country's decision to attack Pearl Harbor, which killed 2500 Americans and destroyed 18 ships. The US declared war the next day. Over the next few months, Japan captured British-occupied

Singapore, Dutch-occupied East Indies, the Philippines, New Guinea, and other regions in Asia-Pacific and Southeast Asia.

However, the tide turned against Japan in the Battle of Midway in June 1942, and by 1944, they realized that victory was unlikely. However, Japan did not stop fighting until atom bombs were thrown on Nagasaki and Hiroshima in August 1945. On August 15, 1945, Emperor Hirohito announced Japan's surrender to the US through a radio broadcast.

Emperor Hirohito after WWII – A postwar constitution set up by General MacArthur preserved the monarchy in Japan but reduced it to mere symbolism stripping it of its 'divinity.' Many of his top military leaders were tried and indicted as war criminals. However, Emperor Hirohito himself was spared from being tried as a war criminal because the US were worried such an act would hinder the Occupation process.

During the occupation period, Emperor Hirohito toured all over the country and supervised reconstruction processes. After the end of the American occupation in 1952, Emperor Hirohito remained in the background as he watched his country make gigantic strides in economic growth and development. He died in 1989 after serving as the Japanese emperor for 64 years, the longest in the country's history. Even today, his reign is controversial and is a matter of debate among historians and scholars.

Hirohito's tomb

Japan's Journey to UN Membership

Within a decade after being defeated in WWII and facing the humiliation of US Occupation, Japan was invited to join the United Nations in 1956. It was a remarkable turn of events, indeed, for Japan. The countries that set up the United Nations against Japan, Germany, and Italy were the ones who were inviting Japan to join the gang because these same countries (Britain, the US, France, and China) now viewed Tokyo's membership as an advantage.

The political scenario had changed considerably since the end of WWII. Cold war brewed across the globe. The Korean peninsula was divided and was in a constant state of war.

Central Europe perceived an ideological/military standoff with the Soviet Union. And, in the midst of such turmoil in Asia, Japan with its pro-West and democratic stand was viewed positively by the UN. Japan was expected to be a key element in multilateral diplomacy across various countries in the United Nations.

The year 1956 was the year that Japan received the UN invitation. That year consisted of multiple geopolitical events, which changed our world as we knew it until then.

In October 1956, Hungary revolted against the Soviets in a brave and bold move. During the same time, the Suez Crisis happened which involved Israeli, British, and the French forces trying to wrest back control of the Suez Canal from Gamal Abdel Nasser, the nationalist ruler of Egypt.

However, the stage for entry of Japan into the UN was actually set when the Peace Treaty was signed in September 1951 between the Allied nations and Japan. Delegates from 48 Allied Nations (except China and the Soviet Union) had signed this Peace Treaty giving back independence to Japan. Interestingly, the Preamble of this Peace Treaty signed in San Francisco had the following declaration, *"Whereas Japan for its part declares its intention to apply for membership in the United Nations."*

For a country to gain membership in the UN, the recommendation of the candidate country should be made by the UN Security Council to the General Assembly. The threat of vetoing Japan's membership request was from the Soviet Union, which held an antagonistic political relationship with Japan.

However, Japan seemed to have the full support of the US right from the beginning. The State Department, in 1952, issued a Confidential Memorandum that clearly stated its goal to secure Japan's admission to the UN at the earliest date possible. Japan made a formal request for membership in June 1952. The then US President Dwight Eisenhower and his administration supported Japan right through the complicated journey of securing membership to the UN. The fact that Dwight Eisenhower was reelected in 1956 helped matters.

In the year 1955, there was a surge of membership to the UN with 16 countries being recommended by the Security Council. Fourteen of these 16 countries were part of a package deal with nine non-Soviet applications (Ceylon (present-day Sri Lanka), Austria, Italy, Ireland, Jordan, Libya, Portugal, and Nepal) and five Soviet applications (Bulgaria, Albania, Outer Mongolia, Hungary, and Romania).

As expected, a Soviet veto against membership for Japan created a criticism sandstorm in Tokyo. However, Tokyo's turn came the following year. In October 1956, a diplomatic agreement between Japan and the Soviet Union was reached wherein Moscow said it will support Japan's request for UN membership.

There was a nagging concern that the USSR might wrangle something from Japan in exchange that would be unpalatable to the West. The diplomatic breakthrough took some time in coming, and in December 1956, the Security Council agreed to recommend Japan's membership request to the General Assembly, which voted unanimously on December 18, 1956, in favor of the recommendation.

Today, Japan is a key player in the United Nations and is the second largest financial contributor to the UN system.

****

Can you help us?

If you enjoyed this book, then we really appreciate if you can post a short review on Amazon. We read all the reviews and your feedbacks will help us improve our future books.

If you want to leave a private feedback, please email your feedback to: feedback@dingopublishing.com

Thank You..

****

Conclusion

The current period in Japanese history is called Heisei, a name given by the present Emperor Akihito, after the death of his father, Emperor Hirohito. Heisei translates to 'peace everywhere.'

The year 1989 was one of the most rapid economic growth stages in Japan. A strong yen, a favorable yen-dollar exchange rate, and low interest rates sparked an investment boom in the country. Property prices in Tokyo skyrocketed, and Nikkei 225 reached an all-time high of 39,000. By 2015, Nikkei 225 had fallen to 15,000 reflecting the decline of the Japanese economy.

By 1988, the Liberal Democratic Party, which was ruling the country unchallenged for 38 years, was losing its appeal among the people, thanks to many scandals and scams. In 1993, the LDP lost the elections, and a coalition government headed by Hosokawa Morihiro was elected to power. However, this coalition collapsed because the parties were not unified in any other social and political issue except to oust the LDP. The LDP returned to power in 1996.

The '90s was marked by some terrorist attacks and natural calamities too. The Kobe earthquake happened in 1995 and a sarin gas terrorist attack took place in Tokyo's subway system in the same year.

The Heisei period also was a time for the re-emergence of Japanese military powers. However, constitutional bindings prevented the Japanese from participating in the Gulf War even though they pledged billions of dollars to support it. After the war, however, minesweepers from Japan went to facilitate the reconstruction work in the Gulf.

The Yoshida Doctrine that was so successful in pushing the growth of Japan during the post-WWII era was grappling with challenges in the 1990s. Protectionism and large trade imbalances brought on a lot of pressure from outside the country to eliminate unfair trade practices. And within the country, the Japanese companies with a global presence wanted policies that gave them workforce flexibility and open markets to bring in foreign goods. Moreover, during this time, Japan began to feel increased international pressure to share the world's military burden.

Emperor Akihito

He was born in 1933 and his original name was Tsugu Akihito. As per the Japanese tradition, he is the 125th descendant of Emperor Jimmu, the legendary first Japanese emperor. Akihito is the first son and the fifth child of Emperor Hirohito and Empress Nagako.

His early years were spent as a student learning and undergoing training in the traditional imperialist way in the schools reserved for nobility. After the end of WWII, when his father's rule was reduced to a ceremonial title, his education expanded to include the study of the English language, and learning and understanding the Western culture.

In 1952, he was given the title of the heir to the Japanese throne. Seven years after this ceremony, Akihito broke tradition and married a commoner; a first in the history of Japanese imperialism. He married Shoda Michiko, the daughter of a wealthy businessman. They have three children, and the eldest, Crown Prince Naruhito was born in February 1960.

Emperor Akihito ascended the throne after the death of his father, Emperor Hirohito, in December 1989. He gave the name Heisei to his reign, which roughly translates to 'achieving peace.' Emperor Akihito and his empress wife have traveled the world as ambassadors of Japan.

He gave his first televised broadcast in 2011 when a tsunami and an earthquake destroyed northeastern Honshu. This natural disaster resulted in the death of over 20,000 people and caused one of the worst nuclear disasters at Fukushima Daiichi Power Plant.

In August 2016, he addressed his countrymen again hinting that he was ready to abdicate the throne giving reasons of declining health and his inability to continue doing his duties. This address was an appeal to the Japanese lawmakers to alter and include a clause to the Imperial Household Law of 1947, which defines the line of succession.

This law did not specify what would happen if an emperor was to abdicate or retire. In June 2017, the Diet passed a special law that allowed Emperor Akihito to abdicate and hand over charge to his son, Crown Prince Naruhito. The entire process has been formalized and the exchange of power is to take place on April 20, 2019, when Emperor Akihito will step down and hand over the Imperial Court duties to his eldest son.

Today, Japan is still a global power despite not-so-encouraging economic growth figures and trade deficits and credit problems. The people of the country are known to be one of the most hardworking races in the world. Perfectionism is not just a norm but an obsession in the country. Large Japanese conglomerates have a global presence.

The modern-day Japanese is trying to balance ultra-modern luxury with age-old customs and traditions even as he or she works hard to keep the Japanese flag flying high.

Bonus

As a way of saying thanks for your purchase, we're offering a special gift that's exclusive to my readers.

Visit this link below to claim your bonus.

http://dingopublishing.com/bonus/

More books from us

Visit our bookstore at: http://www.dingopublishing.com

Below is some of our favorite books:

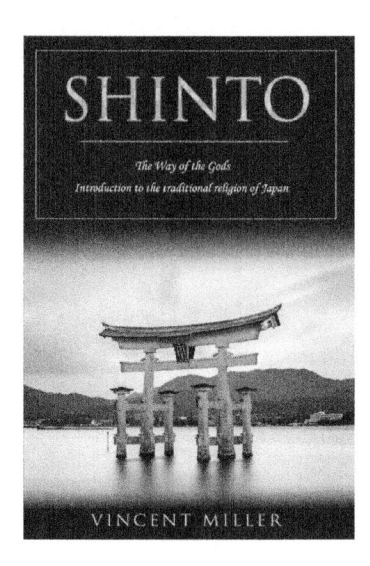

SIMPLE, HEALTHY AND DELICIOUS CHIA SEED RECIPES TO LIVE LONGER AND FEEL YOUNGER
CHIA SEEDS
Cookbook
Superfoods Every Day
Olivia Green

THE TOP 99 DELICIOUS RECIPES TO FIGHT CANCER AND RESTORE YOUR HEALTH
ANTI-CANCER
Diet
Olivia Green

LIFE IN VIETNAM
The Essential Guide for Travellers
MICHAEL LE

RAMEN
NOODLES COOKBOOK
The Top 50 Delicious Ramen Recipes To Cook At Home
LINDA NGUYEN

Book excerpts: Japanese Etiquette
The essential guide to Japanese traditions, customs, and etiquette

By: Vincent Miller

Chapter 1: The Use of Names

One of the most important elements of Japanese etiquette is to be aware of how to address people and how to use names in different social and business settings.

Addressing People with Respect

San is a commonly used respectful expression that is put at the end of people's names while addressing them. San can be used when using the first name or the last name of the concerned individual. Also, san is used for all people irrespective of marital status or gender.

Sama is a term that is more appropriate in a formal setting and is to be used after the family name. Also, you must remember that you must use san or sama after everyone else's name (whom you wish to show respect to) but not after your own name. Here are some examples of the use of san and sama:

- Smith-san (Mr. Smith)
- Michael-san (Mr. Michael)
- Sandra-san (Ms. Sandra)
- Smith-sama (Mr. Smith again but to be used in a formal setting only)

- Tanaka-sama (Ms. Tanaka)

Another way of respectful address is by using the job title of the person along with his or her name. This works in a scenario where you need to address your superior at work or your teacher at school. For example, you can say Brown-sensei (Brown teacher; sensei is teacher in Japanese) instead of saying Brown-sama. Or bucho-san which is referring to your department head; bucho is head in Japanese.

In business environments, using surname instead of given or first name is more respectful. Use of one's job title instead of their name is also well accepted in Japanese business circles. This subtlety of using surnames instead of first names might come across as a bit stiff for some non-Japanese. However, you must remember that most Japanese are uncomfortable using first names.

However, there are a few Japanese citizens with a lot of exposure to Western cultures that have come to accept being addressed by their first names. Some of them have taken this even further and have created nicknames for themselves, which they embrace happily. You can use these nicknames too along with san or sama depending on the level of formality of the setting.

The final tip here is to remember that you can never go wrong using the surname with the san or sama suffix. For all else, it would be prudent to ask around and then make a sensible choice of addressing the concerned person. The convenience of san cannot be underestimated considering that it is unisex and, therefore, you don't have to worry about how to address people through email especially if the Japanese names are not clearly gender-specific.

Also, if someone is addressing you with the san suffix, accept it as a compliment. That's the intention of the Japanese name-calling etiquette.

Addressing Family and Friends

In Japan, addressing family members and friends also calls for politeness and respect though there is less formality than the use of san or sama. There is a plain form and there is a polite form when it comes to addressing family and friends. Here are a few examples:

- Otto or goshujin – husband
- Tsuma or okusan - wife
- Okoson – child in a polite form and Kodomo – child in a plain form
- Otosan – father in a polite form and Chichi – father in a plain form
- Okāsan – mother in a polite form and haha – mother in a plain form
- musukosan – son in a polite form and musuko – son in a plain form
- musumesan – daughter in a polite form and musume – daughter in a plain form
- otōtosan – older brother in a polite form and ani – older brother in a plain form
- onēsan – older sister in a polite form and ane – older sister in a plain form
- imōtosa – younger sister in a polite form and imōto – younger sister in a plain form
- tomodachi – friend

During conversations, shujin is used to refer to one's own husband and otto is used to refer to someone else's husband. Tsuma is used to refer to one's own wife and kanai is used to refer to someone else's wife

Here's the trick when it comes to using the plain form or the polite form. If you are addressing an older member of the family, then you must use the polite form. When addressing the younger members of the family (spouse also comes in the category), you can use the plain form. To get this right, you must also know the difference between referring to someone and addressing someone.

Referring to someone means you are not talking to the person but are referring to him or her in a conversation with someone else. Addressing someone, on the other hand, is talking to the person directly.

Commonly Used Japanese Expressions

While we are at this, let me also give you the top five commonly used expressions in Japanese conversations:

Yatta – I did it! – You can use this term whenever you have accomplished or been offered a great job or have won something. All these occasions can be classified under the 'Yatta' category.

Honto – Really? – This expression is used to let the person speaking to you know that you are listening to what is being said.

Â, SÔ DESU KA – I see – Also, a conversational bit of phraseology letting your partner (the one who is talking to you) know you are getting what is being said. A nod invariably accompanies this expression.

Mochiron – of course! – An expression of confidence

Zenzen – not at all – a phrase of emphatic denial (in a polite way) used for situations such as when someone asks you, "Am I disturbing you?" and you politely say, "zenzen."

Chapter 2: Greetings and Body Language Etiquette

There are many ways of greeting people when you meet them. This chapter is dedicated to these Japanese greeting methods.

Bowing

Bowing, or bending at the waist level, is a form of appreciation and respect shown by the person who is bowing to the person who is being bowed to. Bowing is a common form of greeting used along with:

- Good morning - ohayo gozaimasu
- Hello, good afternoon - konnichi wa
- With words of apology or gratitude (arigato)

There are three types of bows depending on how deep the waist is bent. These three types include:

The casual bow (eshaku bow)

Bending at a 15-degree angle, the casual bow also entails a slight tipping of the head. The eshaku bow is used when casual greetings are passed between people or when you pass someone belonging to a higher social status. Casual greetings in the form of good morning or good afternoon or thank you are sufficient by themselves. Yet, when used along with the eshaku bow makes the greeting more heartfelt.

The business bow (keirei bow)

This bow entails bending your torso at 30 degrees and is used when entering and/or leaving a meeting or conference or while greeting customers.

Deep bow (saikeirei bow)

This is the politest form of bowing in Japan and entails lowering the torso by 45 degrees. It is used to express very deep feelings of regret (apology) or gratitude.

Clasping Hands (Gassho)

Bringing both the palms together and clasping them in front of the chest is referred to as gassho. This form of greeting has its origins in Buddhism. Today, it is used before starting a meal and after finishing the meal along with the word, 'itadakimasu.' The word, 'itadakimasu,' means to receive or to accept an item or gift. It expresses gratitude for the food and for the person(s) who prepared the meal.

Bye-Bye

While 'sayonara' is the Japanese word for saying goodbye, the phrase 'bye-bye;' is also commonly used in the country. There is a subtle difference in the way the hand gesture works with sayonara. While in the West, you would open and close your palm as you lift your hand, in Japan, your open palms are waved from left to right and back. The hand is lifted high above your head so that the other person can see it and then the open palms are waved from left to right and back in a broad arch. The eshaku bow is also used commonly while saying bye-bye.

Shaking Hands

Although bowing is the more appropriate Japanese form of greeting, the handshake has come to be an accepted form of greeting, especially in a business setting. However, it is important to note that the handshake of the Japanese is far limper than the 'firm handshake' of the Western culture. This is easy to understand considering that the Japanese culture does not allow for too much physical contact, especially in public.

Body Language Etiquette

Nodding is an important gesture in Japan. When you are talking to someone, it is important that you nod often to imply comprehension. Your nod is telling the speaker that you are listening to him or her, and you are understanding what the person is trying to say.

Silence is an accepted form of nonverbal communication. There is no need to chatter merely to keep a conversation going. Silence is, in fact, an expected means of communication. Talk only when addressed or when it is your turn to do so.

Standing very close to a Japanese person is considered rude and uncomfortable. Avoid touching as much as possible except for that first handshake (the bow is a better option).

Making prolonged eye contact when talking to someone is also considered rude in Japanese culture.

Hugging, shoulder slapping, and other forms of physical contact are also to be avoided, especially in public. The Japanese frown on any outward show of affection of any kind.

Using your forefinger to beckon is disallowed. The Japanese way of beckoning calls for extending your right arm and bending the wrist in the downward direction. You are not allowed to beckon any person older than or senior to you.

How to Sit Correctly

Sitting in Japanese style calls for sitting on the floor and in an upright position. Even meals are had while sitting on the floor with low tables for the food. For tea ceremonies, it is mandatory to sit on the floor.

Both genders use the kneeling, or the seiza, posture to sit in a formal environment. It can get uncomfortable after some time for people (especially Westerners) who are not used to this way of sitting. In modern times, foreigners are exempted from sitting on the floor. In fact, many modern Japanese also find it difficult to sit like this for long. In casual environments, it is common to see men sitting cross-legged and women sitting with both their legs to one side.

If you are sitting on a chair, you are expected to sit with both your feet firmly placed on the ground. You cannot cross your legs or place your ankle on the knee while sitting on the chair.

The seating order works something like this: the most important person (usually the customer or the guest) is furthest away from the door. The place that is farthest away from the door is considered to be the good side in Japanese culture.

If there is a tokonoma (an alcove decorated with a hanging scroll accompanied by a flower arrangement), then the guest is usually placed in front of it. The least important person or the host takes the place closest to the door.

Also, in a business environment, all the people from the same company are seated on the same side of the table. When you visit Japanese businesses, it is common for the receptionist to show you your seat. If you don't see this happening, it might be prudent to ask before taking a seat.

************** End of sample chapters **************

Thanks again for purchasing this book. We hope you enjoy it

Don't forget to claim your free bonus:

Visit this link below to claim your bonus now:

http://dingopublishing.com/bonus/

www.dingopublishing.com